# DRIVING THE BIRDS

## Jabonkah Sackey's Story

A bush girl's escape from her heartless father,
ritual mutilation, and mission slavery.

# Russell Traughber

Shadwell
PUBLISHING

Shadwell Publishing
info@shadwellpublishing.com

Book cover graphic illustrations, design and photography provided by
Robert Sabin of Sabin Design Studio, P.O. Box 3237 Idyllwild, CA. 92549
rsabin@sabindesignstudio.com

ISBN: 0615621570
ISBN 13: 9780615621579

# Acknowledgements

Thank you, Jeanette (Jabonkah), for the privilege of bringing your childhood story to life. I admire your courage and your desire to share your story with others with the hope that the women and girls of Africa might become one-day closer to living lives of self-determination and freedom from female genital mutilation and abuse.

Jeanette and I thank our supportive friends who aided in bringing DRIVING THE BIRDS to print:

Ruth Siebert, Judy Fancher, Gaynel Kendrick, Kathryn Jordan, Marian Tully, Annette Harden, Frank!, and Gail Heisel.

Jeanette and I would also like to thank our children (Jeanette's: Kwame and Nefatiti and mine: Nathan, Kurtis, and Garrett) for their understanding: Jeanette for her need to share her story and me for my need to write.

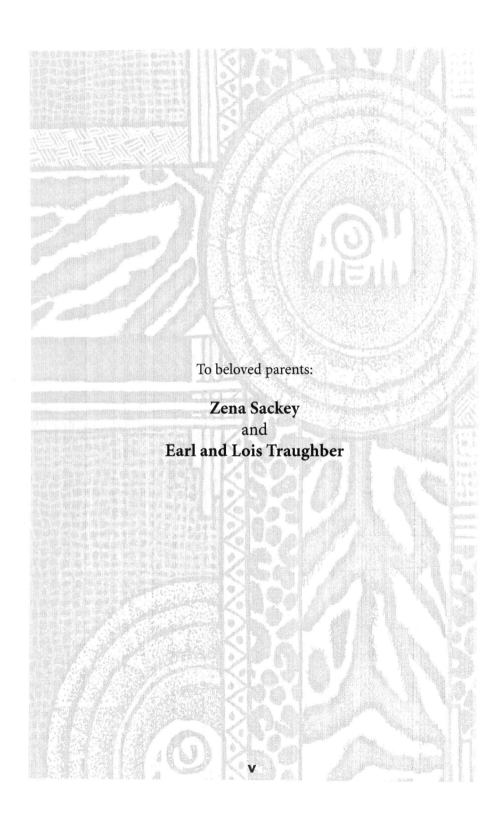

To beloved parents:

**Zena Sackey**
and
**Earl and Lois Traughber**

# Table of Contents

# Table of Contents (Continued)

# Prologue

Welcome to my story. My African name was Jabonkah Sackey, and my American name is Jeanette Mills. I have endured the weight of Jabonkah's hidden truths for too long, and I have chosen to set them free; just as Jabonkah wanted to live—free in body and in spirit.

Over the years, I've been told that my story ought to be shared. But I was not ready then; and once I did start, I quit. Recounting my memories was too painful. But later, after a period of reflection, when I considered the African girls and African women who still lived in mud huts in isolated villages and who were graduates of "the Society," I tried again.

Then weeks later, I'd read several of the initial chapters and began to sob. I had to stop once more. In the written word, Jabonkah's world came to life: the isolation of the bush, my village, the sound of the drums, and the people I loved—and hated. Reading these pages forced me back to a time when life was so painful, nearly unbearable.

My reluctance to share was not just about me and my fear of sorrow. I wanted to protect the dignity of my beloved mother, Zena, and hide the shame of those who should have loved me, who should not have abused and enslaved me. Ultimately, it was Jabonkah's courage and strength that squared me to the task of embracing my childhood, "the good, the bad, and the ugly."

I am Jabonkah! I am eight years old. My story begins in a mud hut deep in the African bush, forty miles from Monrovia, the capital city of Liberia. The year is 1956.

# 1

# Black Rooster

The black rooster sang his first song of the day, repeating it again and again and again. Father had tried to kill him many times, but the young bird was fast and alert for danger. Father thought it was bad luck to own a black rooster. I was left handed, so he thought that I was a witch and also bad luck. He probably wanted to kill me, too.

I lay with my eyes closed beside Zena in her bed. My fingertips roamed her back. They explored the smooth scars from old beatings and gently traced crusted wounds that were yet to heal. My father, John Henry, beat her with the brass buckle of his belt. He beat her for things I did. After all, he told Zena—she gave birth to me. He also beat me.

I wished Father dressed like the other men in our village, bare chested with skins around their waists. They had no belts. Instead, Father wore a white shirt and long, dark pants, which required the belt. He was also different from the other men in our tribe. He was very tall, very black, and very mean.

"Why does he do this?" I said.

Zena pulled my hands from her back and pushed me to the side of the bed. She brought her fingers to my lips. "Shhh. He hears you. Go wait by rice hut."

"Too early," I said with a sleepy moan. I rolled back to her and wrapped my arms around her neck. I pressed my face against her breasts. They were as smooth as the red mud of the river bank.

Zena tried to push me away, but I held tight and said, "Mama Kama sleeps with Father. She makes his food."

The night had not cooled. Our shared sweat soaked us. I pressed my ear against her chest and released it, making popping sounds.

"When I'm a woman, will my breasts be small like yours or big like Grandma Crowcoco's?"

Zena poked a finger in my side. I laughed and turned sideways to avoid a second jab. She attacked my ribs with all of her fingers, saying, "You drive the birds today."

This meant that it was the first day of rice harvest. I sprang from the bed and grabbed her hands. I tugged and tugged. "Hurry, Zena." The smell of freshly cut rice was like nothing else. "Come, Zena! Get our food, but avoid Father."

She quickly got up and pressed her hand over my mouth. She whispered, "Shhh...John Henry hears you." I nodded, grasped her hand, then turned her palm to my nose—lime. After she bathes, which is far too often, she cuts limes in half and rubs the juice under her arms. I stopped adoring the scent and said, "Why is Father so cruel?"

Zena took her hand away and used it to lift my chin, wanting me to look at her. She hid her eyes from all others but never from me and Grandma Crowcoco. The first glow of morning shone on her face. Her deep dimples were like holes in her cheeks.

"John Henry rules. Why question him?" she said, then pulled me close. She rocked me side to side, slowly, as in my earliest memories. She whispered into my ear, "Too many words, Jabonkah, too many words." She released me. "Now go."

With Father in the other room, I knew it was best to leave through the window. Zena patted my bare bottom as I climbed out. The ground was still dark. I stepped carefully. Sharp ridges were everywhere, created when others in my village had walked in the mud from the recent rain. Their feet made depressions in the mud, and when they dried, thin, sharp edges surrounded them. I tested each step to avoid pain in my arch, which was more sensitive than the rest of my rough and calloused foot, should I tread on anything.

I was also alert, while walking in the dark, to avoid stepping on snakes, especially those that had just eaten. They moved slowly, bulging in the middle, sliding to their nests or a branch to digest a big, fat frog, rat, or smaller snake.

Father began to shout at Zena. My steps slowed even more. Sometimes I covered my ears when he yelled at her and when he beat her. He never had a good reason, and listening to his mean voice never explained why he was so cruel. But this time I had to listen. I didn't want Father to stop us from going to his rice field, the biggest one of our tribe. I stood and rubbed my itchy nose. I was near the corner of the rice hut, where Zena had wanted me to wait.

Father yelled, "Don't forget my lunch, and don't send that left-handed witch."

I switched hands and rubbed my nose with my right hand. His voice was as tall as he was. He was always demanding something, often speaking with anger, especially when he included my name among his words. "Why should we have to interrupt our work in the field to take Father his lunch? He could take his own food and eat it cold," I said to myself.

I squatted to pee, listening for the sound the buckle made on Zena's back, hoping not to hear her sad cries as she swallowed her pain.

# 2
# The Smell of Rice

Father's buckle made no sound on Zena's back. Her voice made no cries, and I would have heard both from the corner of the rice hut. I relaxed. The heat from my pool of pee touched on my soft edges. My smell mixed with the dirt and the rice dust that spilled from the mouth of the big hut.

"John Henry—"

Zena's unsure voice called Father's name, then he stopped her words like he always did. He never wants to hear, only talk. I stood and listened for Father's very angry voice that would mean trouble for Zena. I was relieved he was only using his normal upset voice that only hurt your ears and not your back.

Zena always called Father, John Henry. Zena told me not to call her Mother but to call her Zena, because we were more like sisters. She was only fourteen rice fields older.

Grandma Crowcoco said to me many, many, many times, like I'd forgotten after the first time, that when Zena had given birth to me, her breasts were too small to keep me from crying. Grandma Crowcoco said

I would want more than Zena had, so she had fed me with her milk. Her breasts are still big, but now they are flat and hang on her chest like empty rice sacks.

Zena said we were like best friends, not mother and daughter. We played together and worked together, and we somehow knew what the other was thinking. This was easy for Zena, because as soon as a new word was born in my head, my mouth opened and the word flew out, along with many others that must have somehow stuck to the first one. Zena hardly ever talked. Once I asked her why she spoke so little. She told me I took all of her words when I was born. I think this must be true. My mouth always seemed to flow with words like the rapids of the rainy season. But it was also easy for me to know what Zena was thinking, because her eyes and face had voices that said things, short things but filled with many seeds of emotion.

I rose to my toes, stretched my arms high, then opened my hands, pointing to the waking sky with all my fingers.

"Good morning, sun, and good night, stars."

I came down from my toes, then ran along the smooth path to the place where we had our largest fires. I jumped into the air, flapping my arms like the blackbirds that were flying from the treetops into the orange glow to meet the lazy sun. I yelled at them. "I'm going to the rice field today with Zena, so stay away, or I will drive you off."

I stopped flapping my arms and watched for Zena. Yellow spears of sunshine drove away the darkness from my village and gave my hut a golden glow. I wondered what was taking her so long.

Mama Kama would see that Father had his white shirt and his breakfast of rice, dried fish, and cassava greens. Father had three wives, and they took turns making Father happy, which worked most of the time, but he could create a storm from the steam in a bowl of soup.

Father wore his white shirt to the iron-ore mine where he worked, but he never got dirty like the miners. I didn't understand why he was different, and I didn't care to know. I left him to his world and wished he would just leave Zena and me to ours. I didn't need to be ruled like Zena was; I didn't understand this, except she'd had more beatings than me. Maybe someday, he would rule me, but I doubted that.

I ran into Father's rice hut, the largest in Bomi Hills, back where Zena wanted me to wait. Here was where we'd store the bundles of rice stalks that we would cut today. It was nearly empty of both the bundles and the smell of rice. But this would change very soon. Zena and I, my aunts and uncles, and others—but not Grandfather, because he was blind—would work for many days, cutting the rice, tying the fallen stalks into bundles, then carrying the bundles on our heads from the field to the rice hut. Later, men would work together like ants to make tall piles that would not fall over, even when I climbed on them, which I was not supposed to do.

After we finished the harvest, the rice hut would be so full that I could climb to the top and touch the ceiling. The hut was also a place to hide from Father's anger or to sleep when ants filled our hut or to listen to the rhythms of the rain or to escape when it was Zena's turn to be with Father.

The best part of harvest was the smell of rice. I loved the smell of rice. The machetes cut the stems and released a fragrance that filled me with a joy that was as big as the sky and as beautiful as a rainbow. I didn't understand why others didn't roll in the cuttings like me. The adults and other children didn't seem to care. If my nose were to grow as big as my head, I still could not have breathed in all of the fragrance I craved.

"Jabonkah," Zena said, just loud enough for me to hear.

I jumped in the air, opened my arms, then spun around on the smooth floor of the rice hut. But when I saw Zena carrying only one bucket of food, my stomach growled me to a stop. I guessed Father was too angry for her to get enough rice for two meals, or he had questioned why she needed so much to eat for just herself and me. I ate a lot for someone so small, Grandma Crowcoco always told me. I calmed myself by telling myself that I didn't care if my stomach was empty, because soon I would be in the rice field with Zena, breathing in and filling up an empty part of me that was hungrier than my stomach.

I ran to Zena and hugged her, careful not to make her spill the water. I let go of her waist and reached for the bucket she balanced on her head.

"No, take machetes."

"But I'm good at balancing now."

"A large bucket?" she said. Her eyes narrowed at the corners.

"No, Zena. I might drop it, and we would have no water for a long day."

I ran to grab the machetes from the dark corner of the rice hut. Returning to her, I walked slowly and carefully. Zena had taught me how to carry sharp things, and I remembered. Before she first let me carry knives, she told me a story about the boy who ran with a machete, tripped, and fell on the sharp blade. It split his stomach open and some of his insides came outside. He died later. Zena said that little bugs called germs killed him. I don't think we have those kinds of bugs in my village; at least, I have never seen any, and I can see really small bugs.

"Look how careful I am," I said.

Zena gave me the look: eyes opened wide, lips pulled back, and dimples deeper set than at any other time. She approved.

"How do we know the rice is ready to cut?" I said.

"John Henry knows."

"How does he know the rain will stop, so we can cut the rice?"

"He knows."

I thought about this for a moment, then I said, "But it's not fair that we don't understand. What if he was dead? What would we do then?"

Zena didn't answer. She looked ahead.

The narrow path divided the thick, green brush. Tall trees grew above our heads and hid the morning sun. Monkeys jumped from limb to limb, rattling small branches and screeching to scare us away from their territory. Leaves fell around us as we walked. I didn't recognize these monkeys, so I didn't talk to them. My monkey friends lived in the trees along the road to Bomi Hills and above the path to the river.

"I will ask Father how he knows the rice is ready to cut," I said, "and he should give me the answer."

We walked in silence until I spotted a wall of yellow hibiscus. I hurried ahead, careful with the sharp blades, holding them by the handles away from my legs, not swinging them, watching each step for roots that might snag my feet or vines that might tug at my arms. I ignored the monkeys, birds, and snakes. I even let the biting flies taste my blood. But the hibiscus I could not ignore. The blossoms were the size of my two hands, and the bush they grew on was so thick with flowers, it seemed like a big yellow blanket.

I waited for a large brown snake to pass. I was not allowed to jump with the machetes. The snake had a big bulge in its middle. Once, I had tried to swallow a whole piece of cucumber without chewing. I screamed like a wet monkey, and Zena hit me many times on the back, but that only made my back hurt. The cucumber moved slowly down my throat, and it felt like I was being cut from the inside. That was the last time I did that.

The machetes clanked when I dropped them. I gathered a handful of flowers, drove away a bee with a puff of my breath, then drew their softness to my face. I closed my mouth and eyes and breathed in long and deep, enjoying the sweet centers, where tired bees liked to rest. I nibbled a small rabbit-sized piece of petal, because I knew it would taste bitter. It was almost as sour as a lemon. I didn't understand how something that smelled sweet could taste so terrible. Nobody else knew why either. And when I'd ask people, they would just look at me, like when they saw me break off clay from a hut wall and eat it. I stopped asking about how something that smelled good could taste bad, but I never stopped wondering.

The bee returned with another bee friend, buzzing near my ear. They reminded me I was going to the rice fields. I plucked the flowers I had gathered with a tug, then rubbed them on my cheeks and neck in slippery circles, hoping the sweet smell would last on me as the lime did on Zena's fingers. I looked back for her. She was not there. She was ahead of me.

I ran and waved the knives just like the men of the village did as they danced with their spears. I leaped and jumped just like the skinny monkeys did if they were caught on the ground with a panther chasing them.

I yelled, "Zena," running as fast as my legs could go on an empty stomach.

Zena stopped and turned. "Walk!" she said.

Getting to her, I stopped, dropped the machetes, then grabbed her around her middle. To my eight rice fields, Zena seemed like a giant, but Zena was the smallest of the adults of my village. She continued to hold the bucket that held our lunch, so she hugged me with one arm.

"I'm sorry, Zena." Her body was stiff. I lifted my head from her chest and exposed my neck. "Smell me." She hesitated. She put down our lunch can and the water bucket, then bent down and sniffed around, tickling my neck with her snorts. She stopped searching and drew a long breath. Zena moaned a little, which made me happy.

"Why doesn't Father hug me when I hug him?" I said.

She pulled away, opening her eyes. "He is John Henry." "Why don't you hug Father?"

"He is John Henry."

That seemed to make sense, and I didn't care to understand more about my father. The sunrays were pale yellow through the bright-green trees, and the smell of rice was waiting for me. We were still a long distance from the rice field. I let go of her waist and ran ahead.

"Jabonkah, the machetes."

I stopped and ran back, grabbed the machetes, then said, "Hurry, Zena."

I ran again.

"Walk!"

I slowed, a little.

The trail ended at the rice field. I dropped the machetes where Zena could find them and skipped along on the bank, which ran around an area bigger than our village. Usually the bank held the water in the field, but now the field was dry.

I yelled, "Fly away birds, or I will throw sticks at you." The sparrows took flight all at once, in one body, confused it seemed and undecided where to go, but they stayed together. They were the easiest to drive away.

The blackbirds continued to hop along the bank, jerking their heads left and right, staring at me, wondering, I thought, if I meant what I said. I charged them, yelling with my loudest voice, "Fly away. Fly away." They jumped and flew, reluctantly, not all at once like the sparrows. Blackbirds seemed to have minds of their own. Each flew when it wanted to, but I made certain that they all wanted to.

I jumped from the bank into the field. Tall stalks of rice surrounded me. I reached up and looped my arms around the stems, bending them toward me in a hug, careful not to snap the stalks that had become brittle because there was no more rain. The rice at the top, nearest my nose, smelled the strongest. The music of the bush—a lone bird crying out, parrots arguing, and the locusts clicking their wings against their bodies as they flew—disappeared as I entered a total existence of aroma, refreshing my worn memories of the last harvest.

"Jabonkah," Zena said, calling for me.

I climbed the bank and looked for her. I spotted her cutting the first stalks. I ran, waving my arms in the air, yelling at the blackbirds, which were not afraid and didn't listen. I thought of Father's belt and how I might use it on them; if I had it, I would swing it around my head in circles, showing them that I ruled. I rushed along the bank, flying in the air, at times, like the birds, flapping my arms and wishing I could fly. I called out to my aunts and uncles as they approached the field. They seemed less happy to see me.

I tumbled and fell into the cuttings at Zena's feet. The blade of the machete had released a clean, crisp sweetness that made my mouth water.

I rolled and rolled and rolled over the stems Zena had cut and would later bundle.

She hummed as she worked but never sang. She must have heard me moaning from my pleasure. She looked behind her. "Drive the birds, Jabonkah."

But this experience that only came once a year was like none other in my life—the rice field seemed as one great flower, and its fragrance filled my head, as satisfying as all of the dumboy I could eat or as exciting as the thought of Father never returning home. "But, Zena, I am still hungry for the smell of rice."

She fixed her eyes on me, arms folded across her chest, a machete pointed to the blue sky. "Drive the birds or they eat what you not have."

I rolled to my back, sat up, then found the blackbirds pecking at the fallen stalks and their clusters of grain. When the stalks stood, the ends were too weak to hold the weight of the heavy blackbirds. They knew to wait for the rice to be cut to the ground.

Angered that they ate my rice, I sprang to my feet and ran in expanding circles until all of the birds had taken flight, then I hurried to where one of my uncles gathered the fallen cuttings. I hid there. Zena would not see me, and my uncle would not bother me. He, like most others, thought I was a witch.

# 3
# Christmas

After rice harvest, we celebrated Christmas. This was when I wore my special dress that was dark blue and had red embroidery and bits of white. I had a matching hat. Our village and neighboring ones, which were also part of the Gola tribe, expressed our happiness for an entire week, making this a very memorable time.

At Christmas I looked like a girl rather than a short skinny boy. Life in the bush required few clothes for children. Year round, I wore a flap across my front. I could have worn more clothes as did most of the children who lived in Bomi Hills, where my father worked, but I would just get them dirty while learning to be a bush woman like Zena. She wore more clothes than I did but somehow she didn't get them dirty. I think dirt liked me. I liked it, too. Zena didn't like dirt, and when she could catch me, she tried to scrub it away with soap and a brush you could scale a fish with. Christmas was the only time when I was willing to lose my scales to the brush.

Our drums filled the air with sound, joining other Gola villages that spoke the language of our mouths and beat the rhythms of our ears.

Drummers who lived across the river, those who lived close to where the sun hides, and those who lived where the sun shows its face at the beginning of the day, joined my village. Together they made thunderous echoes that seemed to bounce off the white clouds in the day and the stars at night, never seeming to stop, telling of our endless joy in one great celebration.

The people of our village gathered around my father's fire, the largest of all others. He owned many huts, and people paid him money to live in them, or they worked in his rice fields. I lived in Father's biggest hut. During the gathering of men, from all the Gola villages, my father always had much to say, and the others seemed to listen.

During this time of celebration, Father removed his white shirt, long pants, and buckle. He dressed like the other men, wearing skins across their fronts and paint on their bodies. He joined the men in their dances and stood the tallest and strongest of all.

The men drank palm wine and pretended to be the brave hunters our people had once been. Dancing men grunted and jabbed at animals that you could not see and that were larger than the animals I knew. They had killed so many animals by the end of the night that they seemed to fall over them, but I knew they were just drunk.

This celebration was unfair. The boys painted their faces, chests, and arms and were allowed to dance with the men. They even took gulps of palm wine. The men didn't care, and although some mothers wanted to protest, they didn't. As the night grew long, the men became drunker and unable to stand. This was when the women were allowed to dance. The older boys refused to dance with the women. I danced beyond the endurance of my legs. The girls always outlasted everyone else.

The women had painted each other's faces and shared beads. We joined hands and made a circle around the fire, dancing to the same rhythms as the men, expanding away from the blazing heat, then tightening back again as we sang, chanted, and cried out to the night.

While dancing, I was free of the man's world. I felt the power to rule over myself, and I felt the acceptance of the other women and the girls of my tribe. Best of all, I was no longer left handed, an outcast. I moved to the sounds of the beating drums, receiving the smiles of other women and girls as if they were gifts.

Christmas was also a time for feasting. There was rice, dumboy, cassava, sweet potatoes, greens from both the cassava and potato plants, and all sorts of meat: dried fish, chicken, monkey, wild boar, and sometimes fresh cow meat—all this was mixed in varying combinations that were roasted above a fire or slow cooked underground or, my favorite, deep-fried in palm oil.

As much as I loved to dance, I loved to eat even more. At Christmas, there was always more than enough food to satisfy my hunger.

# 4
# Left Handed

After our Christmas celebration, Zena and I practiced making me right handed. The night before, Father had tied my left arm behind my back— his solution to the curse the devil had given me. My bed was a matted bunch of scratchy palm fronds on the floor in the corner near the entrance to our hut. I fought all night long, refusing to sleep, straining against the cords, determined to pull my arm free. Dawn finally came, and I was still bound.

Zena was with Father. He yelled at her about how she should do more for him without his having to ask. Mama Kama, Father's first and head wife, was most likely in her room asleep. Zena was the second wife. Father's third wife didn't live in our hut.

My contempt for Father had multiplied to a new level during the night. I had not cried, and I had refused to accept physical pain. Zena had been in pain many times and didn't complain, so I tried to be like her.

I lay motionless, tired beyond sleep, listening to Zena prepare Father's breakfast, still determined not to allow him to rule me as he did others and Zena. In my mind, I saw him dressed in his white shirt, dark-gray trousers, and black shoes.

He had tribal roots but dressed as the white men did where he worked: the Liberian Mining Company in Bomi Hills, which was a short walk from our hut. I supposed that the walk took about the same time it takes a small snake to swallow a big rat. That was in the dry season. In the wet season, it was a long, muddy irritation for Father to walk to work or come home. After Father left for work, Zena came to me.

"I hate him," I said, clenching my teeth.

Zena didn't respond. She coaxed me onto my side and untied me. She brought my arm to my front and inspected it. A bloody groove circled my wrist. She placed my hands in my lap, sat me up, and then moved behind me. She rubbed my left shoulder. The sharpest pain grabbed at the insides of my throat, clawing it, like when I had swallowed the large piece of cucumber. I fought back tears. Zena's tender rubbing could not reach the roots of my anger. I closed my eyes, seeing her fingers in my mind. They seemed to be under my skin. She pressed against the stiffness of my muscles and coaxed them to give up their anger.

"I hate him more than before," I said louder.

Zena said nothing. She often spoke to me in this way—silence. After my rub, she took me outside and sat me on a log. She went inside and returned with a bowl of rice and a piece of salted fish. She also had a damp rag.

I jammed in mouthfuls of rice and fish. Zena dabbed the bloody ring and scrubbed away the blood that had run down my left arm. She took advantage of this time and cleaned more than she needed, scrubbing the skin on my back.

I turned to look at her. "Do you think I'm a witch?"

She shook her head.

"Why does Father think so?"

She continued to care for me in silence. She had thoughts. I know she did. But she seldom shared her words unless she was frustrated with me.

"Well, if I'm a witch, then I curse him to the most horrible pain, stabbing pain, the agony of many spears entering his body from all sides." I drew a choked breath and shuddered. "He is *never* sorry when he hurts you or me." The pain in my left shoulder was almost gone.

"The man rules," Zena finally said.

"Why? Why should he?! You and Mama Kama do all of the work. All he does is eat and—"

"Jabonkah! Too many words," Zena said.

I turned to her. With both hands, I reached over and stuck an index finger in each of the holes in her cheeks. I pulled my fingers away from her face and poked them into my dimples. "We are the same person. You must hate Father, too. Don't you?"

"Man rule. Woman work. John Henry rule. Zena work." She lifted my right hand and held it in front of my face. "This one. This one serves John Henry."

Last night I had served Father his food, as I had seen Zena do many times, but I had used my left hand. He knocked the bowl away and called me a witch. He dragged me by my arm and threw me into my corner. He ordered me to stay and left the hut. I felt as if I were a crumpled and empty rice sack, meaning no more to him than the many other rice sacks he owned. He returned with a cord and tied my left arm behind my back.

"I tried, Zena, but I get nervous when I'm around him, and I forget."

Her alert eyes, clever as a monkey and alert as a panther, were as black as the night. She said, "We use soft cord. You learn."

Zena left me to finish my breakfast, and then later she made a loop with a ribbon she may have cut from an old dress. She wrapped it above my sore wrist, and then tied the ends around my waist. Throughout the morning, she handed me different things, and when I felt the tug of the binding, I reached with my right hand. We repeated and repeated and repeated this until I made no mistakes and used my right hand every time.

Next we went into the house. Zena sat on her heels in Father's chair so she would be taller, like him. She tried to appear angry as Father always seemed to be. She narrowed her eyes, crossed her arms, and clenched her teeth, so her jaw muscles bulged. Then she surprised me. Zena banged on the table and said in a loud voice, similar to Father's, "Bring food, woman."

We both laughed. I ran to her and jumped in her lap. We hugged. I took her face in my right hand and said, "Let's go away from here. Let's go to another village, even if it's a different tribe. We could learn their language."

Zena stopped laughing and seemed disappointed. "He find us. He owns us."

"Not me!"

Still holding her face, I began to kiss her all over as she squirmed and laughed. Finally, she said, "Stop...stop. We practice now." And we did.

I brought Father's bowls and cup on his tray to Zena, while she sat and tried to look mean. We practiced until it was time to take Father his lunch. Zena dished rice, dumboy, and fish soup. She covered the tray with a white cloth. She draped that with a red cloth, which she tied to each corner. I took the tray from the table.

"No. More practice." Zena latched onto the tray's other end.

"But I want to go alone to show Father I'm right handed. I can do this. Please, Zena, please."

Zena held firmly, equaling my hold, not trying to take the tray away but not allowing me to have it. She shook her head. "You not ready."

"I'm better. You said so. Please, Zena. Let me try. I know I can do this. And what's another beating? My back can have many more before it looks like yours." Her eyes escaped to the floor. A sudden pain hurt me as I had just hurt Zena. "But your front is beautiful and you are the best bush woman—and mother."

With nervous effort, Zena lifted the edges of her lips into a smile. She nodded. She let go of her end of the tray. She reached across the platter, grasped my shoulders, and then turned me toward the entrance to the hut.

"Put left hand behind you. Then, serve John Henry."

I nodded repeatedly and said, "Thank you, Zena. I will do it like that."

She released my shoulders. "Don't be confused."

Zena was right to remind me. Wonderful distractions of the bush filled my senses: to watch, to smell, to hear, to taste, and to touch. People liked me, but now, looking back, I realize that the children who lived in Bomi Hills liked to tease me. I was different from them. The adults liked to talk to me, probably because I said funny things in response to their questions.

"I won't," I said to Zena. But, as I turned to walk away, I began to worry that I might be late taking Father his lunch; I was so easily distracted.

# 5

# Father's Lunch

I walked on the road to Bomi Hills to take Father his lunch. The skinny monkeys jumped from limb to limb and tree to tree, following me, screeching at me in monkey language.

"Not today, my monkey friends. I'm taking Father his lunch, and I can't be late or I'll feel the buckle on my back." With their squawking voices they told me about their disappointment that I did not stay and play. Their voices reminded me of unhappy chickens when I chased them for Zena to catch one for us to eat.

"I promise to find you termite bark on my way back." But they kept talking and talking and talking. Monkeys always complain when they don't get what they want. I would have covered my ears, but Father's tray was in my hands.

I became angry at the monkeys the more they complained. They made me have thoughts of setting the tray down and having fun with them. These thoughts made me worry that I might not be ready to take Father his food. I wanted to run from them but could only walk faster.

"Shut up, you stupid monkeys!"

After a short distance, I came to a clearing and the small rice field of another Gola village. I spotted a big, red tomato among the green rice stalks. Shiny and fat with juice, it weighted the vine, bending its branch, threatening to split it from the stem. The fruit almost touched the ground, and that would spoil it.

"Please eat me before I rot," it said to me.

I said to it, "I want to help you, but I'm taking Father his lunch, and if I'm late, he has a belt with a buckle that is hot and hard when it hits you."

I worried more that I was not ready to take Father his food. Ignoring the talking tomato was difficult. It was so red with flavor and so fat with juice. I hurried away but took several looks back, careful not to spill the soup, trying to forget a great thirst that I hadn't even known I had until I saw that fat tomato.

Houses appeared as I got closer to Bomi Hills. There were fewer huts like the ones I lived in. The huts were among houses that had doors and windows with glass. Other differences between my tiny village and the town of Bomi Hills were the children and dogs. The kids had better clothing, not that I cared, and the dogs were fatter than those in the bush. Perhaps smelling Father's lunch, two dogs followed me: a white dog with brown patches and a black one.

I turned the street corner and saw four girls leaning against the wall of the market. One called out to me. "Jabonkah, where is your mother? Are you lost?"

I wished I had seen them before they noticed me. I would have taken the long way to the mine where my father worked. These girls were not nice. In the past, they had teased me and Zena. All were bigger than Zena and, of course, bigger than me. After I came near them, I said, "I'm older now, and I'm taking my father, John Henry, his lunch."

They straightened, walked into the street, and then stood in front of me, blocking my way. The oldest and tallest, Martha, reached to remove the red cover from the tray, but I jerked it away. Warm drops of soup spilled through the tray bottom and dropped on my feet. I tried to walk around the girls, but they shifted positions when I did.

"My father will be angry with me for spilling his soup. Please leave me alone."

"My father said your father is building a kingdom," Martha said. She might have been thirteen or fourteen rice fields.

I didn't understand what she meant. "Is a *kingdom* a town with many houses, like yours?" I said.

The girls giggled, and when they stopped making themselves happy, Martha said, "John Henry doesn't come to you every night, does he? So, where do you think he lives when he is not in *your* hut?" She made the word "hut" sound like a forbidden word.

This is the same question I had asked Zena, but she would never answer. For days he would not return to Zena, Mama Kama, and me. And because he didn't come home to give us money, sometimes we ran out of palm oil or other things that we bought at the market. "Do you know where he stays?"

Martha pointed to the youngest girl, who was maybe six rice fields. "He stays with Victoria's mother. John Henry is *Victoria's* father," Martha said.

Victoria wore a pretty dress and had two bright strands of beads around her neck. I only had one old strand. I was used to having halfbrothers but no sisters. I had only known those children of Father's three wives. I felt betrayed, especially for Zena. Now I understood what a kingdom might be. It could be a town full of houses Father owned. I sensed that it was more than this. He probably also owned the people who lived in his houses.

I show them my angry teeth, then said, "Let me by, or I'll tell John Henry it was you who spilled his soup, and he'll come and beat you."

Victoria looked up at Martha with the biggest eyes that said she knew John Henry would beat them. Martha moved her head back and to the side as if she were thinking about something. Although she didn't seem worried, she stepped aside. I hurried past them and didn't look back. I must be late, and Father is going to be upset, I worried.

The old, bent-over man at the gate to the mining company recognized me and asked where Zena was. I told him I was older now. He smiled and let me pass. I opened the door to a huge house where my father sat at a big table. Papers were spread in front of him and also stacked beside him in neat piles. Three white men were also in the big room with Father. They had big tables, too, and papers.

"Hey, Sackey," one white man said, then nodded toward me. I balanced the tray in my left hand and closed the door.

Father looked at the wall and the round circle that had numbers on it, and then smiled at me. "Where's your mother?" he said, in a gentle voice he only used here in this house in front of these white men.

I could not answer, because I was upset about his kingdom and his daughter, Victoria, who wore a pretty dress and pretty beads. I set the tray down on a small table next to the big table, as Zena always did. I removed the red then the white covers. Father made a space among his papers. I placed the bowls in front of him.

I looked up at him. Instantly, my anger about his kingdom disappeared. His eyes fixed on me. Without saying a word, they told me he was furious. I had served him with my left hand. I was not ready! Zena must have known this and let me come anyway, knowing she would get a beating. My heart became sad for Zena.

"Hey, Sackey, that smells good. Too bad that brat of yours doesn't have more hands; she could bring us lunch." They all laughed. Even Father laughed.

Father stood. He patted me on the head, like he had done before, bent down, and then whispered in my ear, "Get back to the bush, you little witch."

My anger returned. "Why, do you have to make a kingdom? You—"

He slapped his hand over my mouth and used his other to grab the back of my neck. I could not breathe or speak. He pushed me in front of him, so the white men could not see, I thought. Father took me outside. He shoved me, causing me to fall.

I ran back to my village and to my Zena.

# 6
# Boiling Water

On my way home, I ran past the four girls who were still at the market. They laughed at me and called me a stupid bush girl. Martha's voice was the loudest. I ran fast and stopped at the small rice field where I had seen the fat tomato. I bent over and took several deep breaths, and then I plucked the fat tomato from the vine. I ignored the monkeys' screeches, yelling at me much like the girls had. I continued to my village and to Zena.

When I got there, Zena was not by the fire cooking or in the hut. She must be at the river, perhaps washing clothes. I ran along the twisting path. Thick brush and low-hanging limbs shaded me. It was much cooler than the dry, hot road to Bomi Hills. I closed my mouth, and I ran through a cloud of gnats, waving them away with my right hand.

Zena and Grandma Crowcoco were walking toward our village, carrying baskets of wet clothes on their heads.

"Zena, look what I found for you." I held out the tomato in my left hand.

She stopped and crossed her arms. I lifted the red fruit higher and closer to her face, in case she had not seen it.

"John Henry angry?" Zena said.

The tomato became heavy. I lowered it to my side. "He acted as he does when he's with the white men, nice and thankful, but…he hid his voice from them, and he called me a witch for no reason."

Zena and Grandma Crowcoco stood looking at me. I suspected they didn't believe. They knew, somehow, that my words didn't tell the truth. They waited. I brushed my foot back and forth in the powdery dirt. "He forced me outside and pushed me down where the white men couldn't see," I said, still not wanting to tell them what had really happened.

Zena looked at the rut I'd made with my left foot. "You use left hand. You forgot."

I leaped, dropping the tomato, and wrapped myself around Zena. After a long pause, she slipped her arms out from my hug and gathered me to her.

"I'm sorry, Zena. I needed more practice."

"The darkness cannot be removed from the night," Grandma Crowcoco said, then stepped ahead of us and walked toward our village.

I pushed back from Zena. "Father is building a kingdom. Did you know he has other wives and children in Bomi Hills? How can he do this to us? I hate him—and you should too."

Zena stepped around me. She sighed as she headed for our village with the dripping basket on her head.

"Why must it be this way?" I shouted. "It's not fair to have so many wives…and…and children who have nice dresses." I looked at my empty left hand. "Three wives should be enough!" Zena didn't stop or turn to respond.

The tomato had split open. Greenish pulp and yellow seeds were trapped inside a reddish juice bubble that floated on the ground. I used my big toe to press on the single eye staring at me. I popped it. Juices flowed and spread, then vanished into the ground.

"Zena! Wait!" I ran and caught up with her. "I will take your beating. It's my fault. Why should you be punished for my mistake?" She began to hum as she did in the rice fields, yet I knew she didn't have the same feeling of happiness. "Zena, why don't we run away?"

She stopped, turned, and faced me. "John Henry rules, and you—too many words!" She twisted her face and stared at me as if this explained everything. Of course it didn't—until I saw a puddle of tears in her eyes. We stood with the gnats around our heads and birds screeching in the trees. We shared the same soul. Our eyes each entered the depths of the other's. She opened her arms. I entered the only place I was accepted and loved.

Cool water from the basket on Zena's head dripped on my back. Tears slipped down my cheeks.

"He will beat us tonight, won't he?"

"Tomorrow, we dig cassava."

I loved the cassava fields, because I got to dance on the monkey bridge and got to be with Zena for the whole day. I thought about how I would sway and bounce as the river flowed under me, and how Zena would sit and watch me play before she went ahead to the field.

She took my hand and said, "It was beautiful tomato." She led me toward our hut and resumed her humming, squeezing my hand now and again, and reminding me that she loved me.

The rest of the afternoon and early evening, I sat on the edge of the big stone mortar. The pestle rested between my drooping legs. I leaned forward against the black wood and placed my chin on its handle that rough hands had made smooth. My arms dangled to my sides. I must have looked like a dead turtle. I kept watch for Father's tall figure to appear on the road that connected his work with our village. Zena had finished cooking his supper of rice, cassava greens, fried fish, and dumboy.

She brought food and sat next to me. She eventually left, but sometime later, a village dog approached slowly, gathering courage, creeping. Its tongue drooped to the side, tail between its legs, ears folded back, avoiding my stare, sniffing and desiring to lick the bowl Zena had brought me, which only had the smell of food left. He got the bowl, biting it on the edge. He held it in his mouth and began to crawl away.

"No!"

He dropped the bowl and ran. If only he could ask permission, I might have allowed him to take what was not his.

Finally, Father appeared. He was easy to recognize. He was the tallest man I had ever seen and skinny but powerful, especially when he grabbed you. I slipped around the pestle and ran up to him. I wanted Father to see how fast I could run. I ran especially fast, as if thunder and lightning chased me, like when God is talking to you; at least, this is what Zena said about all that noise and light.

Just before I got to Father, I skidded and lost my balance. Little dirt balls rolled under my bare feet. Father caught the top of my head, preventing me from falling into him. I pushed forward and grabbed his legs. I hugged him, tightly. I wanted him to feel how strong I was.

He had never hugged me back. Zena says, "That is John Henry," and this is why she hugs me so much. I looked up at him. His eyes scared me. They focused on me with the full strength of his anger. He was going to beat Zena and me. He hit me on top of the head with the bamboo tray and said, "Get off me, leech."

I released him. He took a swipe at me with the tray, and I ducked. I ran faster than I had run to greet Father, to go warn Zena. She must have known I was not ready to be right handed, but she had let me try anyway. It was my fault—again. She had never done anything to deserve Father's punishment, but I had.

I shouted as I entered the hut. "Father is angry."

Zena was at the window. She had been watching. She turned to me. She had changed into a dress she had worn to the fields many times. I walked up to her, out of breath. All I could do was look at her. Her smile was strained. Her lips twitched at the corners, her eyes in motion. They darted to the entrance, then back at me.

"This is my fault, Zena." I grabbed her hands and tugged. "Let's run away."

She jerked free. "Where to?" She gazed out the window, rubbing her palms on her thighs. "Go to my room," she said.

"No."

"Please, Jabonkah."

I shook my head.

She bit her lower lip, placed her hand on my shoulder, and patted it. Finally, she said, "I fear for you, not me."

"But, Zena, how can I leave you?"

She drew me to her chest, and we waited as if a storm we could not outrun was about to overwhelm us.

Father filled the entrance with his body. Zena tried to push me behind her. I resisted, but she was much stronger. She stood between Father and me.

He flung the tray at us, but we ducked. "You sent that witch!" He pointed a long finger at me. His deep voice filled the hut.

I was used to being called a witch, but it never hurt like it did now. I slipped in front of Zena before she could stop me.

Father took one large step forward and struck me on the side of my head with his open palm. Zena caught me. My left ear sang a song like I had never heard.

He pushed me away from Zena. He choked her, lifted her, drove her toward the table, then shoved her against the edge. She doubled over. Her face was very close to his supper.

He gathered the bottom of her dress and yanked it. He forced her to straighten, exposing more and more and more of her body until he had her dress in his hands. He made a ball with the cloth and threw it across the room. Zena gripped the sides of the table. Her knees were shaking. The scars and the gashes on her back made me sob with sorrow. I jumped between them. I laid my body against Zena's naked back.

"No, Jabonkah!" Zena said.

Father yanked his belt off with a snap. The buckle hit my back, driving my breath away. My back burned and ached where the metal had struck. I cried out. He grabbed me by the neck, lifting me off my feet, and flung me against the wall. I collapsed and burst with pain. The buckle pounded Zena's back, the sound dull and hollow. She gasped. I flinched as if I had been hit again.

He struck her twice more before I could grab his swinging arm. He turned on me, raised his arm, and then circled the belt in the air. His belt hit me, and the buckle landed against the side of my head.

Great ringing, pain, and small twinkling lights flashed in my dizzy head, and then my knees weakened, causing me to fall to the floor.

Again and again and again, father beat Zena. She whimpered in anticipation of each strike, wheezed when the buckle hit, then moaned with new pain.

"Stop it," I screamed. Zena's back bled bright red. Father turned on me. I scurried far from reach. Zena forced herself to stand against the blows, never begging for mercy. That's when I realized the power Zena had over my father.

I watched each blow in horror. I had to suffer with Zena. I had to be strong for her. I could not allow Father to force from me what Zena would not allow him to force from her. My anger grew until my hatred for Father was complete. I wanted him dead, breathless and cold. He was nothing but a wild animal that must be killed.

After Father had finished, I helped Zena crawl to her room.

Father sat to eat, watching us with little interest.

I strained to lift Zena to her bed. She lay on her stomach.

"I hate him," I said, but she didn't respond. This beating was worse than her last when Father had accused her of sleeping with other men while he had been gone for many days. Of course, Zena never slept with anyone but him. I would have known.

I covered her back with a white cloth that Zena used for our wounds. She soaked the cloths in a bucket of smashed lemons and rain water to remove the stains. The fabric darkened with black-red, spreading in circles under my fingertips. Zena had taught me how to stop bleeding. I used both hands, laid them flat, and pressed with my palms and fingers to stop the blood from leaving her body. There were so many deep cuts. Her flesh moved. I thought chunks might fall off if she were to stand.

"He is an animal," I whispered into her ear. I shook her left shoulder, which had been spared the buckle. Her eyes drifted in dizzy circles, reminding me of a man who had drunk too much palm wine.

"Zena, I want my bath!" Father said from the other room.

I shook Zena's shoulder again and whispered, "Zena." She didn't respond. Father would not stop his demands until he got what he wanted. I walked out of Zena's bedroom, my eyes focused on the floor. I didn't want him to see my thoughts. "I'll do it, Father."

Embers remained from the fire Zena had used to cook Father's dinner. I added strips of dried palm fronds then blew at the base of the rising smoke until a flash of yellow jumped out and stood strong and determined. I fed the fire more wood.

I filled a large, blackened bucket with water and set it on the stones. Flames spread around its sides. The wood popped and crackled. Smoke rose. He came outside and went into his bathing hut. I hoped Father had not noticed the strength of the fire.

The bathing hut had three walls of the same metal that was on the roof of the rice hut, and it had a door made of wood. Father would enter and sit on a wooden bench, which had legs that sat on flat stones. Father had brought these stones in a truck from the mine where he worked.

He walked from the hut with a white towel wrapped around his neck, his maleness dangling like a snake from a limb. He draped his towel on the side of the bathing hut, left the door open, and sat on the bench. His back was exposed.

Zena knew how strong to make the fire and for how long to heat the water to please Father. So did I, but I grew the flames stronger and waited longer. I squatted and slipped more wood under the bucket and into the fire. I looked over my shoulder at Father's back, knowing what I wanted to do, wondering if I could actually do it. Then, I noticed Zena's blood on my hands.

"Jabonkah, don't heat the water too long!" Father said.

"Yes, Father. I have helped Zena many times." The first steam rose. That's when Zena knew the water was hot like Father wanted it. I waited for the first bubbles.

"Jabonkah, what are you doing? Overheat the water, and I will give you the belt."

"Don't worry, Father. I'm a good bush woman." I stared at the bubbles. I held back my tears for Zena, wondering if Father might die. Could this kill him? Or would I die if he didn't?

The metal, looped handle was too hot to hold. I took dirty rags, one for each hand, and lifted the bucket of boiling water.

I stared at the angry water and felt the blistering steam on my face. I would do this for Zena. Father ruled Zena—not me.

"The water is ready now."

"Then hurry."

I walked up to him, careful not to spill the skin-peeling water on my chest. Tears flowed for my Zena who lay on her bed, barely alive. I would do this. I focused on his muscular back and the bumps of his spine. He bent over, doing something with his feet.

He sat up. Just as he began to stand, I threw the bucket along with the water. The water emptied in a wave and spread across his lower back.

He screamed.

I ran.

I think I was out of my mind, because all I remember was running toward the rice field, as if being chased by a herd of wild pigs. Father yelled, "I will kill you if you ever come back here."

This would not be the last time I had wanted to run away, but Zena would never leave our village. I thought our lives had to be better if we escaped. But at the time, I didn't understand what Zena knew: There was no place we could run where father would not find us and reclaim us as his property. There was no abuse hotline Zena could have called. There were no phones. There were no churches to secure refuge for her and me and Grandma Crowcoco and Grandfather. Monrovia, the capital city of Liberia, was forty miles away. There were no "bush" police, and, if there had been, they would not have been concerned about a man who beat his wife and child. Zena was right. The man ruled. He was a king.

# 7

# A Special Place

I don't recall how badly I burned Father or how long it took for him to heal. But I remember the beatings, for Zena and me, were more frequent than before. Perhaps this is why I have no memory about his misery.

One night, as I lay on my bed of dried palm fronds, I heard Mama Kama speaking to him in Father's room. Zena was in her own room, weak again from her latest beating.

Father said, "That girl will not amount to anything. She always wants to be with Zena."

"Let her be. She's a good worker," Mama Kama said.

"Yes, but I don't need another bush woman. Another mouth to feed." He paused. "Besides, she's a witch. And for what she did to me—I am taking her womanhood away."

"You told me she would not go to the Society," Mama Kama said.

"So what. I have other ideas now. She is no good to me, only trouble."

Father exhaled. His breathing became relaxed and mixed with soft moans. What Mama Kama did for him to change his mood made me curious.

"I want her…to go to the Society…the sooner the better."

They spoke no more. Father breathed heavily. He sounded pleased, something I had never made him. In the past, I had wanted to please him, but no longer. He began to grunt, sounding like a pig instead of a man. I had seen monkeys, birds, dogs, and chickens do this to each other. It was interesting to watch animals, but I didn't want to see or hear Father. I covered my ears. I hummed a dancing song until it was over. Father soon began to snore.

The next morning, Zena and I worked outside, preparing rice for cooking. She seemed stronger, which made me happy. I told her what Father had said to Mama Kama about taking my womanhood.

"Is the Society bad?" I said.

Zena used the pestle to loosen the kernels. I shook the flat board and tossed the rice in the air, winnowing away the hulls in the hot breeze.

"It's someplace special," Zena said, but she focused on the grains in the mortar.

"It didn't sound special when Father spoke to Mama Kama. He was angry. Didn't you hear him say he wanted to take my womanhood away?" I dumped the smooth rice into a bucket. "What is my womanhood? What does that mean? Do you have your womanhood?"

Zena scooped a double handful of rice from the mortar and blew away chaff. "All young girls go," she said as she emptied her hands onto the board that I held out for her.

"You don't look happy for me, like when we bought my Christmas dress. Wasn't that special?"

"Tend the rice. Too many words," Zena said, shaking her head.

"Have you been to the Society? Does Mama Kama have her womanhood?"

Zena stopped. She rested the pestle against the side of the mortar. She scratched an insect bite, which had made a bump on her neck, then grabbed the pestle and made strokes that seemed too hard; probably crushing the rice, I thought.

"Did the Society make you feel special?" She hid her eyes. "Why aren't you answering me, Zena?"

Zena raised the pestle high. I thought she would come down hard, but instead she placed the pestle across the top of the mortar and opened her arms. I set the winnowing board on the ground and rushed to her. Holding me tight against her chest, she said, "I be there. That make it special."

I sensed she held back the truth, and she had never done that. She seemed afraid for me, which made me more anxious. I would have to be careful with this thing called the Society.

Soon after I first learned about the Society, and near the end of the day, two men drove a big, green truck into my village.

"What is this?" I said to Zena, who was standing beside me. We had come out of our hut to see why even the lazy dogs were barking; then we heard the truck before we saw it.

The men jumped out, came to the back of the truck, then let a sideways door swing down. There were lots of girls, whom I didn't know, sitting in the back, huddled together. I suspected they were from other Gola villages.

As I looked around, several young girls and their mothers from my village went to the truck.

"You go to Society today," Zena said, with a voice that tried to be happy but was not.

"I'm not ready to go…and Father is not here to make…me…" But there was Father with his white shirt off, like he did in the deepest heat, ending his walk from work.

"You go. No fight John Henry."

I knew there was no fighting Father, but running and hiding seemed like a good idea.

"You not run either." Zena grabbed my arm. "No good." Her eyes jumped to Father's figure and back to me. "Maybe he kill you today."

I released the tension in the arm she held. "You said you will be with me. Will you be?"

"Yes, with you."

The men helped me and the other young girls climb in the back of the truck. Zena turned away.

"Zena!" I called out. She didn't look back but ran to our hut.

"Jabonkah, she sees to John Henry's needs," Mama Kama said. "Leave her alone."

Inside the truck, we sat on benches and were hidden by a cover that smelled of spoiled oil; it spread side to side and over our heads. Most of the girls were older than me but only by two or three rice fields; only two seemed younger.

The truck shuddered violently as it traveled along the rough road that led deeper into the bush. The girls who sat near the end scooted back and clutched together for fear of bouncing out. The seat had wood splinters in it that pricked my hands as I held tight. One of the younger girls latched her skinny arms around my waist. Dust and fumes from the exhaust made us cough and sneeze. My stomach felt sick and my head dizzy.

Some girls cried for their mothers, but none cried for their fathers. Perhaps they understood what taking away our womanhood meant. I was frightened, but I refused to cry.

We drove farther, I thought, than the distance to Monrovia, which was a two-day walk. As we headed deeper inside the bush and night came, we passed no village fires that I could see. The truck slowed for deep holes or sharp turns, making less noise. It was then that I heard screaming monkeys. We had awakened and frightened them.

The truck finally stopped. It had been a long ride. A fire blazed behind the shadows of three women, strange women—none were the shape of Zena. I tried not to feel betrayed. This was a new feeling between Zena and me. I blamed Father for my being here, but Zena may have told me a lie to get me to come. Maybe she had tried to be with me, but Father had prevented her.

As the driver and the other man unloaded us from the truck, the women walked toward us. Once the last girl was down, the women led us to the fire.

# 8

# The Society

It was a typical night: warm, sticky, and quiet, except the crackling fire, the animals of the bush, and the engine that continued to make noise.

A mound of dried palm fronds had been piled on the fire, creating a blaze so high it seemed taller than the trees that surrounded us. The women, who were at least as old as Mama Kama, must have made the fire strong to cast its light so that the men could unload us. But the flames would soon die, ending its crackling and stopping the rain of sparks that flew up to the sky. Fronds burn brightly but quickly die.

The moon didn't have a face. It was thin and seemed alone in the sky. The truck pulled away with a roar. I wanted to run and jump on. I wanted to return to Zena. My heart told my feet to run, but Zena had told me she would be with me. I had to believe her; not believing would have been too terrible to accept, so I decided to stay.

We followed the women and sat by the fire. A fat woman with a bucket of water walked to a girl, drew a ladle full, then handed it to her. She did the same for each girl. Another woman followed the water woman and gave us a can of food each. The can was the size Zena filled for me when we had plenty to eat. I dipped the tips of my fingers inside and felt the warm rice. I dug out a wad and placed it in my mouth—cassava greens with dried fish. Between hungry scoops, I counted fourteen girls.

Some didn't eat. Others ate slowly. Some hunched over with their heads down. Others looked around at the women serving, at the dark bush surrounding us, and at each other as if for reassurance.

I ate all my food. At least my stomach was happy. One of the women returned and took our cans, then motioned for us to stand and walk, driving us into the darkness. Soon we came to a large hut that wore the fire's dim light. The hut had only one large room. They told us we would find palm-frond mats next to the walls for sleeping. The edges of the hut were dark. We had to search blindly for places to sleep.

Once we had all lain down, several girls began to sob and murmur for their mothers and, now, fathers. If I had allowed myself to cry, I would have only cried for Zena. I craved Zena's comforting hugs. But as the night continued, I also missed Father and his powerful presence. "He was responsible for this," I told myself. "Why should I want him or believe he would help me?" I held my breath to prevent my chest from heaving. I closed my eyes to stop the tears that wanted to jump out of me.

I didn't fall asleep for a long time. Someone kept adding twigs to the fire, restarting the crackling and popping just as my eyes closed. Then an owl began hooting, not caring if I wanted to sleep. If the women were awake, they didn't speak but just fed the fire.

A large bird, maybe the owl, stopped its noise, flapped its wings like an owl does when it has a fat mouse or small rat in its talons.

Bugs crawled over me; drinking my sweat, I thought. Mosquitoes buzzed around my head. I fanned them away from my ears. They seldom bit me. Maybe they knew I was a witch.

Zena consumed my thoughts. I sorted through my memories, smiling at times and crying in silence. Mostly, my chest burned from the separation.

I woke before the others. It was dark. No rooster sang his morning song. I scratched my legs. I stepped carefully, so as not to disturb the other girls. My stomach growled. Outside, a short woman stood near the fire, where another woman prepared food. It had to be Zena. I ran toward the dark figure, hoping my greatest hope.

I called out to her. "Zena." She turned. It was Zena. She had not abandoned me. I ran to her and her to me. She closed her arms on me. I nuzzled into her chest. "You should have told me you were coming later."

She rested her cheek on top of my head and said, "I am here till end."

"You mean the end of the day?"

"No, Jabonkah."

"But I feel special now, so there's no need to stay longer."

"Not for many mornings."

"Why?" I pulled away to look at her. "Zena, I want to go now." She gave me her stern look. She had heard enough. I wanted to say a lot more, but Zena turned to help two women who came with handfuls of cassava leaves, which they would boil.

# 9
# Womanhood

We had arrived last night in total darkness. In the early morning, the grey light of dawn uncovered what the darkness had hidden. This was a very old place. It seemed that the bush wanted to take back as its own what had been cut away from its body. Overgrown shrubs choked the paths. Vines crept over roofs and hung in front of openings, hiding windows and doors. Vines also stretched across the ground in all directions. They wrapped their fingers around the stones of the fire circle. And the trees looked down and watched it happen.

This very small village had separate huts for the girls and the women, and there was a small hut that stood alone, with no windows and a closed door. No one came in or out of it.

We girls gathered dead wood and brown fronds, used leaking buckets to fill two rusted barrels with river water, then pulled the strong vines from the black rocks of the fire circle until the vines were gone and our fingers hurt. After we finished, we bathed in the river. By the time we got back to the little village, the sun was low, and the trees created shadows next to us.

Our mothers gave us food, rice with roasted fish; they must have caught the fish while we girls had been working. The warm smell and taste reminded me of my village food. This made me feel happy but only while I ate it.

Early during that first full night, all the girls sat in a half circle on one side of the fire, facing the small hut, which had vines woven into its frond-covered roof. One woman stood on the other side of the fire across from us. The firelight showed us her face. She said that we were about to take an important step into womanhood.

"My father—" I began as I started to rise.

"Be quiet," a woman said from behind me. She grabbed my shoulders then pushed me down. I sat and crossed my arms.

The woman over the fire spoke, as if she were selling something. I recognized this kind of speaking. I used the same voice when I sold bananas in the streets of Bomi Hills. I was not interested in what she had to sell.

After the woman finished, she led us down a narrow path to a small clearing, where a second fire glowed and revealed a closed wall of trees and thick brushes. The bush seemed to surround this place with no trails leading out, other than the one we were on. There were many women waiting. Zena was among them. They stood close to the entry of this small area. After the last girl had passed the women, they closed behind us. I finally saw another, very small, path that led deeper into the bush, but it was not the direction I wanted to run.

We sat near a small fire, and, within moments, a woman appeared from the path where I did not want to go. She held a torch that released a swirling tail of black smoke; it flickered yellow light on her face in a way that made her seem like she was filled with more meanness than Father.

She reached out and took the hand of the girl closest to her. She pulled too hard, causing the girl to stumble, yet she kept pulling. The girl fell several more times. The path swallowed them, but I continued to see glimpses of the torch. It moved deeper into the blackness until it was finally gone. The rest of us sat waiting, not understanding what was happening. None of us cried, but we gave each other worried looks.

The boys of the Gola tribe went away with their fathers to the bush and returned with scarred faces and bodies. Once they came back, they acted as if the scars had made them men, but I knew they were the same stupid boys. Some seemed more eager to fight. None of the women of the Gola tribe had markings like the men.

A scream crawled over me from the bottom of my back to my stomach. It came from the direction in which the girl and the torch had disappeared. Birds in the treetops cried and beat their wings, flying to safety. Monkeys screeched. The girl's terror-filled cry stopped quickly, but her voice continued to echo in my mind.

Those of us remaining around the fire glanced at each other, now with frightened faces. The whites of our eyes glowed against the light. Mothers stood motionless and seemed unconcerned. Zena didn't look at me. I looked back to our group of girls. The woman with the torch had returned. She led another girl into the darkness. Soon, the girl cried so loudly that the hair on my arms stood up. I began to tremble as if I were cold. Her cry turned into a scream, then her voice muffled, like something was put in her mouth.

The woman with the fire in her hand returned and grabbed me. I cried out for Zena. Zena came running. I grabbed onto her. "No, no. I don't want to go." I pointed to the girl beside me. "Take her."

That girl shook her head and began to cry.

Zena twisted my fingers to remove my hands, but she cried with me. The torch woman flung her arms around my waist.

"Let go of me!"

I had to release Zena to fight the woman. She pulled and dragged me, my feet sliding and digging in.

"My father will beat you!"

She jerked me into the air and tossed me over her shoulder.

"Help me, Zena!"

Every living creature, all the way back to my village near Bomi Hills, must have heard me begging Zena to save me.

This bush woman who carried me was strong and determined. With each step, she pounded the ground, and her shoulder jammed into my stomach, leaving me hardly any breath to yell. I think she twisted her body on purpose, because limbs hit me in the face.

I beat my fists on her back until she gave me a blistering swat on my bottom. I screamed louder. She swatted harder. I began to sob. My life was over after eight rice fields. Zena was letting them kill me!

The woman stopped and made me stand. Although it was very dark, another woman covered my eyes with a cloth that she wrapped several times around my head, then tied so tightly that the skin on my forehead stretched and pinched.

A strong arm surrounded my head with a jolting grip, while quick fingers stuffed a rag into my mouth. I gagged. It tasted of spoiled soap. I lifted my hands to pull it out, but they grabbed my arms and forced me to the ground.

Calloused hands, like Zena's, weighted down my straining body, making me lie face up. They stretched my arms and legs out then forced them down. Cords wrapped around my wrists and ankles. They tied me to something solid. I tried but could not pull free. Spread apart, I thought they would gut me like an animal.

Hands lifted my middle and removed the cloth that had been wrapped around my waist. Naked and staked to the ground, the tails of the rag fell deeper into my throat, gagging me more.

A light came close to me, a second, brighter torch. They were going to burn me, I thought, but they would need dried fronds, bark, twigs, and many logs to turn me to ashes.

Pairs of hands pushed down on my hips as if they wanted to bury them into the dead leaves that I felt against my back. I screamed so forcefully that my throat should have come out through my nose, even with the gag still in my mouth.

Rough hands and angry fingers grabbed between my legs then squeezed both sides of the softest skin where boys were never to touch. The fingers of those two sets of hands pulled on me so hard that I thought they would rip the flesh from my body. A sharp blade cut me on one side! Horrible pain! Again on the other side! *Why were they hurting me like this?*

But they were not done. Fingers searched for something above where my pee comes out. They found it, something tiny, pinched, pulled, then cut. Oh! It was the worst pain of all.

Darkness flooded my mind. I might have died it was so black, until a light returned inside my head, along with my suffering.

"Zena, Mommy," I screamed through the rag. "You did this to me!"

Hot, wet leaves were pushed where I had been sliced. This hurt worse at first, then began to have a soothing effect. I stopped pulling against the bindings. I let the knots in my back relax. Someone untied my arms and told me to lie still. Another girl screamed. Now I knew why.

I wanted to touch the huge hole they must have made in my body, but whoever continued to hold my hands kept me from doing this. The cords around my ankles unwound, but I didn't want to close my legs.

"Jabonkah." Zena's voice wavered, as after the beatings Father had given her. She slipped off my blindfold. "Don't scream, Jabonkah."

I nodded, and she removed my gag.

I reached up and latched onto her face with a frightened squeeze. I tried to sit up for a hug but could not. She leaned over, slipped one arm under my back and the other held my bottom. She lifted me.

Looping my arms around her neck, I said, "Zena, will...I...I be okay?" The light from the many torches only allowed an outline of her face. "It... hurts, Zena."

"This done to me. I not remember. You not remember."

# 10
# The Devil Ate Her

he morning heat woke me. In the trees above my head, monkeys screeched upset words. But they had no pain like my pain. They were making me angry and making my head hurt between my eyes. If I could, I would have thrown hard pieces of clay at them to make them be quiet, and I would have yelled at them that I had sharp pains in me. Never before had I thought about hurting my friends, and this made me angrier.

Zena finally came to me. It was hotter than before, so I must have fallen asleep while I was yelling at the monkeys in my head. She carried me toward the ground where we eat but not against her shoulder. She held me in her strong arms like a baby. I pushed my nose in her underarm and found the smell of fresh lime. Zena had bathed.

I ate on my back with Zena sitting behind me holding me up. I ate little bits of fish and small amounts of rice. More than the other girls whose mothers also helped them eat.

After the other mothers had stopped trying to get their daughters to eat, they drove them like squawking chickens to the river. Zena carried me at first, but I wanted to be like the other girls. I told Zena to let me down. I kept my legs apart and held the soothing leaves against my wounds, which burned and throbbed.

Some girls had red stripes on the insides of their legs. I stopped, turned my knees out, then stood on the edges of my feet. Thin streams flowed down my legs. I felt lightheaded. I lost my balance. Zena grabbed me.

"Will…I run out of blood?" The whites of her eyes, normally as white as the insides of a coconut, were veined with red.

"I give you mine, if you do," Zena said.

I didn't think about how she could do this, but her answer satisfied me. Zena and I continued toward the river where some of the girls sat in the muddy water while others refused to sit. Crying flooded the air like a heavy rain. Eventually, all of the mothers got their daughters to sit, some forcing them, pushing down on their shoulders.

Zena didn't need to force me. I sat carefully. The water, which came up to my waist, was cooler than the hot air and the fire between my legs. The red, my blood, mixed with the browns of the water, twisting together in the current, then flowing away. Once we sat, all the girls stopped crying and became quiet.

As the mud eroded from around my bottom, it tickled, giving me a sense that everything would be okay again. The worst had passed, I reassured myself, and what they had cut away could not have been that important; if it was, it might grow back, like my fingernails and hair. Then a girl screamed.

We all looked at her. Others began to scream. Some stood up, spraying yellow from arched legs. I also had a great need to pee and had been holding it for a long time. Knowing it would hurt, I had decided to never pee again; yet the more I resisted the pressure, the greater my urge became. I held my breath. I let it out. I tried to hum to distract myself, but that lasted a short time. "Zena, hum for—"

My urine burst out like a stream of boiling water, burning the remaining skin off that had not been cut away, so it seemed. I may have screamed the loudest of all. I clasped my hands to hold myself, but I was too sore to touch. It felt as if a nest of wasps was attacking me between my legs. Zena held my back, so I would not slip backward under the water. I twisted to look at Zena, wanting to stop crying for her, so I bit the sides of my tongue, hard. It worked, but the pain continued.

When my flow had stopped, so did the attack of wasps. My hands had sunk into the muck of the river. I pulled against the suction and lifted them. I let the flowing water wash away the mud that clung to my fingers. Flies landed on my face, but I didn't care. Birds sang to make me happy, but this was not possible.

As the morning became brighter, the water felt hotter. Zena went to the bank and sat. She cleaned her teeth with a twig. I knew in my mind that it was Father who had allowed this to happen to me, but it took years to realize in my heart that Zena was also to blame. Now as an adult, I accept that she could not have prevented the Society from cutting me nor would she have. It was accepted, a long tradition, a secret part of our tribe that promised death if we spoke about the Society.

But as I watched her scrape her teeth, I wanted to see how she had been cut, if she even had. If she was not lying to me, I wanted to look. Instead of feeling I had lost something, I felt swollen. I decided to ask her to show me, someday. Then I would know the truth and trust her again.

The mothers began to walk to the river bank. Zena waded in and said, "Stand." She held out her hand, which I took. She splashed water on me, carefully cleaning me, scrubbing the mud from my buttocks and legs.

On the bank sat a bucket of leaves someone had brought while we were in the river. We were in line, and when it was my turn, Zena reached in and pulled out several large leaves. I was already standing with my legs apart. She placed the green warmth against me, softly, then pressed firmly. I let out a sigh. We waited for many moments, both smiling at the other. This was the best I had felt since being cut; now I wanted the food I had not eaten for breakfast.

We girls limped back to the tiny village, holding the leaves against ourselves, walking this time like monkeys, feet far apart and shoulders swaying with our hips. After we got there we ate, and after I finished all the rice and dried fish my stomach would hold, I was ready to sleep.

In the hut where we slept, I lay down, and Zena changed the leaves that covered my wound. She held the new ones against me. Before long, I fell into a dark place where I no longer hurt.

I woke in the night in great pain. Zena was gone. The girl next to me was moaning. She rolled her head back and forth with a slow motion that made the dried palm fronds under her head crackle. Without moving my body, I reached and touched her arm. She was shivering. I stretched as far as possible, given my own pain, and felt her forehead. It was very hot and dry.

She kept calling for her mother, too softly for anyone to hear.

I took her hand and held it. It lay limp like a dead snake. She had no strength. I called for Zena, again and again and again, barely hearing my own voice. Zena didn't come. No one came. I tried to get up, but I hurt too much. I swished my hand back and forth over her face and body to cool her. I knew she needed her mother, or she would die; she needed me to get up but my body was heavy like a fallen tree.

Her lips were dry like the inside of her mouth, drier than mine. At least I could swallow and cry for her and tell her she would feel better when her mother came. But no one cared or came. When the sunlight shone in my eyes, Zena was sitting beside me, and the feverish girl was gone.

"Where is she?"

"Who, Jabonkah?" Zena said.

"The girl next to me," I said and pointed to the vacant mat of fronds where the feverish girl had been.

"The devil ate her," Zena said, as if the devil had the right to eat little girls.

I narrowed my eyes and said, "How could the devil eat her if I was here? I would have heard him crunching her bones...and...there would be blood."

Zena glanced at the space where the girl had been. She turned to me and said with her head tilted, "He ate her in the bush." She seemed serious.

"Will he eat me?"

"No, Jabonkah. I prayed to moon he doesn't."

"Then tonight I want to pray with you."

I quickly forgot about the feverish girl and how sad she had made me. And, without being conscious of it at that time, I was glad it was not me who died but she. In the bush things and people perished without surprise but not without great sorrow. I can still remember the smell. We had kept the dead in our huts in a homemade box that was not opened. With each passing day, the stench became more awful.

People came and paid respects to the deceased, and they wailed and screamed for hours. Sometimes they draped their bodies over the casket. This went on during all hours of the day and night, making this a frightening experience for me as a child. But when the time for grieving was over, we celebrated with dance and food for a week. During the Society, there was no mourning for the girls whom the devil had eaten. They just vanished.

That night Zena and I prayed to the moon, she on her heels and me on my back. The moon's shape reminded me of a thin rind from a slice of orange. I sensed nothing from the curved sliver, yet I asked for my life, not to be eaten, and the lives of the other girls; but what I really wanted was not to be eaten first, if the devil was still hungry. I didn't tell Zena these thoughts; she may have had the same wishes for me. Every night we prayed, but each morning brought another empty place to sleep. Zena had no answer for me as to why the moon didn't stop the devil. She tilted her head and said, "We pray harder." After the devil had eaten four girls, he *must* have been full.

As days passed, I was less sore. And after the soreness was gone, I walked with my legs close together. And, once we could stand for long periods, women filled our heads with instruction: how to boil the cassava leaves so they wouldn't make you ill, how to cook rice, how to cut fish without leaving bones in the meat, and how to wash clothes in the creek, beating them against the rocks. I knew how to do all of these things. I had been at Zena's side for eight rice fields. The other girls had difficulty cutting fish and making fire.

The women also taught us songs, which we sang morning and night. This part was fun, because Zena was with me. And there was plenty to eat, which was also fun.

One night, while we were sitting by the fire, we heard a bell ringing. A woman with a painted face and chest ran from the dark, ringing a bell that dangled from the end of a switch. I looked for Zena. The painted woman made me uncomfortable. I had seen women marked like this at Christmas and on other special occasions, but her solitary presence, the switch, and the bell felt like a warning, alerting us of danger.

The bell ringer demanded we stand and sing the new songs we had learned. She yelled at us. She hit us on the backs of our legs with her stick and bell, forcing us to sing louder. We did, louder and louder and louder, until she forced us to scream the songs. We stood on our toes. I spit out the words of each new song until my throat began to hurt.

All of a sudden, the door to the small hut slammed open, and the devil came running out—screaming the most terrible sound. Its arms stretched longer than any human's arms ever could, and its skinny fingers jutted out as if it would grab and eat us.

The woman with the bell yelled, "Louder, louder." I sang louder than I thought possible.

The devil stopped close to the flames and began shaking dried gourds, which had dangling ribbons tied to them, at us. Through the rising smoke, the fire cast a yellow light on the most hideous figure I had ever seen. It had a large, black head and empty slits for eyes. Its body was covered in brown skins that were frayed and strung with red, green, and blue beads.

The devil stomped and twisted and flung around, then it stood still and swayed to the rhythm of our songs. It seemed our singing held it in a trance.

The bell ringer told us not to look at the devil, but I did, until the bell ringer's switch burned across my back. We sang all the songs we had been taught, over and over and over. I watched the devil from the corner of my eye. It swayed, came to life with rapid dancing, then stopped and swayed again. My fear of being eaten increased as I realized how hungry the devil would be after all of its jumping around.

I sang until my throat burned. One girl stopped singing and dropped to her knees. A quick glance to the devil showed me that it was not interested in the girl who had dropped. I wondered if this was what the devil was waiting for, so I fell to my knees, hoping the other girls would also drop; perhaps, making the devil go away.

The bell ringer came behind me and whipped me, and continued to beat me until I stood and sang loudly. She beat the other girl who had fallen until she got up and sang, which was mostly crying. I became dizzy and felt ill before the devil finally disappeared along with the bell ringer.

Zena and the mothers, who had not been in sight during the appearance of the devil, helped us back to the hut where we girls slept. As Zena rubbed my legs, I wanted to be angry but could not be. We had always hurt together. She was hurting now. I fell asleep quickly.

# 11
# Graduation

The next morning, after we had sung without the devil, Zena and I sat with the rest of the mothers and girls, and we ate. The mothers of the girls whom the devil had eaten returned to the group but sat by themselves. They looked sad to me. I wondered if their husbands hated their daughters like my father hated me.

Zena said, "Now you graduate."

The moon had changed shapes. It had been a thin curve when we had arrived, and now it was the same curve again. Zena and I had prayed each night, but I had felt nothing except soreness in my knees.

I trusted nothing here. New things came with horrible surprises. "Zena, I don't want to graduate. I want to leave. Can we? Let's leave now. We can walk back to our village and eat what we find that will not make us sick. Zena you know what we can eat." I looked up with a hopeful face and added, "Please, Zena."

"This is the end."

"I didn't like the beginning. How could I like the end?"

"After, you return to Bomi Hills."

Hearing Zena say the name of our town did comfort me and made me feel excited to see Father again. Looking back, I had had no concept of his control over my life and his power over the people in my village and the Gola tribe until his rule was absent at the Society, a void that made me feel insecure. At the time, I could not have verbalized this, because I didn't understand. Yet, this was when I first felt how powerless I was in Father's world.

I grabbed Zena's arms. "What about you, Zena! Tell me you're coming to Bomi Hills with me."

"Me too." She hugged me, but I hugged her tighter.

We girls and our mothers walked down the trail past the place where they had stolen our womanhood. I suspected all of the girls recognized this place. A wild boar with his vicious tusks rooted in my stomach. Some girls started to cry. It seemed we were all reminded of that horrible night.

Our squirming bodies had brushed away the decay of leaves and exposed the red soil. A large dark spot marked the place where fourteen girls lost their womanhood. The straps, which had bound our arms and legs to the ground, lay slack without our hopeless struggles. The stakes remained ready. They would be used again and again and again, waiting to hold terrified girls. Perhaps some of the mothers remembered, too, because our whole group slowed and looked and was silent.

Once we passed, we came to a single hut I had not seen before. The morning birds were happy, but I was certain no one else felt that way.

We stopped, and our mothers left our sides. We stood in front of a large object. It was almost as long as my father when he was lying down and maybe three or four times as thick as him in height. A white cloth covered it to the ground, so nothing could be seen.

I heard the bell ringing. I looked back for Zena. She stared toward the small hut, which was almost hidden by vines and bushes. Surely, she would not let me be eaten. How could I return to Bomi Hills in the stomach of the devil? This would not be a graduation. The noise of the bell became louder; it was the painted woman, ringing the bell that dangled from the end of the switch. We began to sing, without being told.

I sang loudly, screaming the words, hoping not to be eaten should the devil appear. We sang several songs before the empty-eyed devil charged from the hut. It screamed at us with its arms spread apart, threatening us with a spear it held in its left hand. Unseen drums began to pound.

The wooden-headed beast stood close to the white, log like object, poking at us as if to kill us if we came near it. The drums stopped, and the bell ringer silenced our singing and motioned for us to sit.

Zena and the other mothers whose daughters were alive came close to their daughters. Zena sat beside me and handed me a bowl of soup. It smelled like nothing I had eaten before. Mothers offered their daughters similar bowls.

I took the bowl filled with reddish-brown goo and meaty lumps. I shook my head.

"Eat," Zena said.

I pulled out a thin piece of meat. It was not chicken or fish or monkey. I flipped it off my fingers.

"Eat or you not graduate."

I shook my head. "Then I won't graduate."

The devil turned its frightening head, and Zena reached in the bowl and took scoops of the strange meat and plunged it into her mouth. From the sour look on Zena's face, she was repulsed, blinking rapidly, chewing little, swallowing quickly.

I put my hand on her shoulder. "Thank you, Zena. I'm sorry but I—"

She shook her head as she looked straight, her eyes fixed on the devil, not wanting to be seen, I thought. She ate my sickening food. And when she had finished, she left me and entered the bush where I could not see her.

By the time Zena returned, the bell ringer was trying to get a girl to jump. The drums had started again, and they beat with increasing noise, waiting for her to leap. The log was higher than the middle of my chest, but I was very short. There was no chance I could make it over. I thought the other girls, who had longer legs, could go over easily. The devil had eaten the two girls who were smaller than me.

The devil jumped and stabbed at the place the frightened girl would land and acted as if he would kill her if she did jump over. The bell ringer flicked the switch behind this poor girl, then began to beat her on the back as if her back had caught fire. The girl screamed as she ran and leaped into the air. She made it over, stumbled, then stood, now facing the devil.

It stood close and growled at the shaking girl. It placed the black tip of its spear under her chin and lifted her head. The devil forced her to look at his face, then turned its sharp point to the ground, lowered its head, and stood still, seeming defeated. The bell ringer threatened the next girl in line, and the devil began to dance again. The drums beat faster and louder.

She jumped sooner, seeing that the devil hadn't killed the other girl. The devil acted the same with each girl who jumped, not hurting them, but I kept shifting to the back of the line. The girls who had graduated clapped in rhythm with the drums. They stood near the devil and didn't seem to be concerned. I was the last one on the opposite side of the white log.

Zena came beside me, "Jump, Jabonkah."

"I can't. It's too high."

"You must graduate."

Zena took me by the hand and led me away from the obstacle. "Now, run and jump."

I shook my head. "I'll walk around it."

"Jabonkah," Zena said, with anger in her voice and on her face.

I ran fast, willing myself over the white-covered object. But when I got close, my legs froze, and my feet came to a sudden stop. I was about to walk around it, but the devil raised its spear. Zena grabbed me from behind.

"No, you go over."

"Why, it's just a fallen tree…isn't it?"

Zena's eyes narrowed and she shook her head. "You must. The devil not let you look. You not graduate."

"But I already peeked."

"Jabonkah." Zena grabbed my hand and yanked me away from the obstacle. "Get on my back." She glared at me.

I had ridden on her before when we had played games. She was strong, and I was small. She bent over for me. I climbed on her, throwing my arms around her neck. She straightened and ran, as if the devil were behind her and not in front. Zena leaped and flew. I looked down as the white sheet passed beneath. The girls cheered and the drums sounded louder than before.

After we landed, the devil came near and put its spear under my chin. I looked at the devil. I had graduated the Society.

We stayed another week, celebrating, feasting, dancing, and singing, until one morning we were told we would be going back to our villages.

Some of the girls seemed disappointed to return. They hissed at the news, but I was happy we were leaving the Society. Zena redid my hair in cornrows and painted my face, bare chest, and arms with white streaks and circles of paint. Finally, she looped many strings of beads over my head.

All of the mothers decorated their daughters who were now graduates of the Society. The drums began to beat again, and we danced. I liked this part of the ceremony. We got to dance for a long time until I was so hungry that I was happy to stop and eat. Soon after our meal, a truck arrived. We climbed into what could have been the same truck that had brought us here.

The trip home to Bomi Hills seemed shorter in the daylight. When we were close to my village, where I recognized Father's rice field, the driver began honking the horn. After the truck had finally stopped, the driver told us to remain in the back. The cover that had kept the sun from us was removed. A group of men surrounded the truck, moving closer, talking among themselves. They scared me, because they looked at us in a way that Father had once looked at some pigs when deciding which one to buy for Christmas. They moved closer.

Strange men stared at us. Father stood among them, not noticing me, I thought. After the bad surprises with the Society, I became frightened as to what this meant.

Some men climbed into the truck to pinch us. But I was soon relieved to see that they were interested in the older girls. They seemed to prefer larger breasts, as they smiled when they touched them. Mine were not even buds. I had the chest of a boy. Once they had finished inspecting, they began to bid on us. Buyers argued with fathers over the price of their daughters as if we were animals.

When the highest number of pigs, goats, and chickens were offered and accepted for a girl, she would climb down and leave with her mother and father, having been sold into marriage at the agreed-upon price and date.

I was the last girl left in the truck. Only a few men remained, looking at me as if I were a bunch of bruised bananas. They talked about me, how small I was and how I had no breasts. They asked if I was the one who was left handed.

My father stood below me. I didn't see Zena. She was probably cooking or had not returned from the Society.

Father kept reducing his price for me until he and this ugly man shook hands. I had been sold into marriage to become this man's wife but not until I was fourteen rice fields, which was a great relief. The price: two pigs, one goat, and four chickens. A large sum, my future husband continued to complain, for a left-handed girl.

# 12
# Monkey Bridge

It was early morning. A smoky haze filled the narrow path that led to the cassava field. Zena carried a bucket of water on her head, and her hands held digging knives and twine, which we had made from the strings we'd pulled from palm fronds. In my left hand, I swung the small pail that held our food in long strokes forward and behind me in rhythm with my steps. The heaviness of our food, rice and greens and meat, made me happy to be away from our village and to have Zena to myself.

In our village, Zena was busy with so many things, things Father demanded be done for him. She washed his clothes, shook them open, then pressed them flat with a metal iron I heated in the fire. Cooking the rice, the fish, and the greens to take away Father's hunger took so much time. But here, in the cool quiet, we were alone. The birds were still, monkeys silent, and bugs that buzzed waited for their wings to dry before they could fly.

Ever since losing my womanhood at the Society, I had been curious about what the Society had done to Zena—and to me. I had seen Zena naked many times, but I had never *looked* at her, like I did when I watched my fingers and knife while cutting into a tomato or peeling a butter pear.

"Please, Zena. Why won't you show me?"

She walked in front, not stopping to answer. Yesterday when she had bathed, I stood on a bucket and looked over the short wall of Father's bathing hut. I asked her to spread her legs, and she became angry. She even yelled at me.

Now she turned her head without stopping and said, "Not to speak of Society."

"Wait. Slow down." I ran closer. "I don't want to talk. I want to see." I grabbed at her then tugged at her dress, trying to get a peek, but her dress came to her ankles.

Zena giggled and turned sideways to avoid my groping hands. "Stop it," she protested, using her arms to push me away and prevent me from getting closer. I darted under her pointy elbows and swiped at her dress again. She jerked so fast, water spilled out of the bucket and splashed down her front. "Jabonkah!"

Her tone of voice made me stop.

"Okay, I will find one of the girls who was at the Society and ask them." Zena's shoulders drooped and her mouth opened. She could not have seemed more surprised if I had fallen from the sky and stood in front of her with two heads.

"Where you get these ideas?" She wiped at the water on her face. "It's forbidden! Don't speak of Society." She paused. Her eyes were big and round. She took a deep breath and let it out. She freed her hands, removed the bucket from her head, then set it on the ground. She glanced up then down the trail, drew her dress to her knees, then sat, pulling her dress to her thighs and exposing her legs but not her hidden area.

She waved at me to come near and said, "Jabonkah," breathing out a long sigh.

I went to my knees and crawled to her. I lay on my stomach, creeping forward. "Spread your legs more," I said. I grabbed her ankles, but she swatted my hands.

"Jabonkah! Wait!" She pulled her dress up to her stomach, then quickly opened her legs.

"What...what am I looking at? There's too much hair."

Zena jumped up. She squatted to lift the bucket, then grabbed the knives and string. She hurried toward the monkey bridge. I took off after her. She looked back and yelled, "The food, Jabonkah." I had forgotten our food.

By the time I had our pail; Zena was way ahead of me. I ran to catch her, shouting, "Why are you angry, Zena?"

She continued to walk quickly, avoiding me, until we got to the bridge. She took the pail from me. I had dropped our food into the river once before. "Don't talk of Society. You swore to silence with fear of death." Her face was twisted with anger.

"Yes, Zena, I will not speak of it again." I grabbed the cords that supported the bridge and swung under them like a monkey swings in the limbs of a tree. "But why must we be cut?"

"Too many words!" Zena glared at me. Her face was close to my face. "Man rules."

Zena moved across the bridge without a sway, a jump, or a bounce. She dropped my knife on the other side. The cassava field was not far. She disappeared down the path, still holding our food, her knife, the twine, and the bucket on her head.

I ran to the middle of the bridge and reached for the highest ropes, stretching my arms to hold one from each side. I jerked my body left and right. The bridge began to sway. I kept pushing and pulling, eager to swing faster. The wind cooled my bare chest and face.

Then I let go of the ropes, stumbling at first. My heart jumped when I realized I could have fallen into the river that was fat with water. Fear made me want to grab for the ropes again, but I found the rhythm of the bridge before my worry grew to panic. I pushed left and then right with the weight of my feet, closing my eyes, sensing the time to push down and when to be still.

At this moment, like most moments before the Society, I was content and happy. My joy grew with the energy of my dance. The trees that surrounded me became a green blur. I was dizzy with delight. I stumbled and fell onto the smooth wood where many feet had passed, making a worn path across the wooden boards. The inside of my head and my eyes continued to spin, so I closed my eyes until my head stopped spinning, then I was ready to start over.

Again and again and again, I repeated a dance that released the rhythms from inside me, which disappeared like a mist into the air. A heavy sensation had entered me and made me happy. It reminded me of the times I was full from eating lots of dumboy or when I rolled and rolled and rolled in the fresh smell of cut rice.

Zena called my name, "Jabonkah." At first her voice and my name seemed part of the other voices in my head—chattering birds, creaking ropes, rushing water—but, as Zena kept repeating it, my name began to sound strange. Zena didn't seem happy to be calling my name; maybe she had been for a long time.

I ran to the other side, where Zena had dropped my knife. The end of the blade was flat, made for digging, but the edge was sharp, made for cutting. I reached above my head and grabbed one of the four ropes that kept the bridge stretched between the riverbanks. I cut it. That side of the bridge dipped. An excitement filled me, like when I had outrun Father when he was chasing me, knowing he wanted to strangle my neck, then beat me. I cut a second. The bridge turned on its edge. I began to cry in anger, not knowing why. I hacked at the third and fourth, blinded by my tears. I cut away the joy the bridge had given me.

My end of the monkey bridge fell into the river, and the current swept it downstream until it tangled. The brown water grabbed the boards and wound them around, around, and around, braiding the ropes into a single strand with a motion that caused my head to feel dizzy.

The ropes bent the trees on the other bank like a great storm pushed them from behind. I wondered what would happen first—would the trees break open, showing their white bones, or would the ropes rip apart with a fighting scream?

My excitement boiled as I waited to see what would happen. The ropes stretched and stretched and stretched as the trees curved then bowed and became crooked like a dog's hind leg. One rope breathed out blue smoke. I blinked several times, not believing what I saw. I felt dizzy and, for the first time, scared of what might happen next.

A terrible snap made me jump. The smoking rope disappeared—some sort of magic was happening that might bring a curse on me. The trees seemed to agree. They swished and jerked back and forth, alive with anger, a warning. I backed away from where the bridge had been. A strange force squeezed out the excitement that was in me and left my body heavy with sadness.

I looked down the path for Zena, needing her but not wanting her to see what I had done. I ran for her, only thinking that Zena could drive those distressing feelings away. Now close, she saw me; she opened her arms. I wanted to crawl inside her body. I hugged her with my very strongest hug.

She had to pull hard to tear me loose. She was laughing, maybe thinking it was a game. "I need help," she said. "Play after work." We worked for a long time as Zena hummed and I listened. We stayed side by side. She was happy now, but she wouldn't be when she saw that the monkey bridge was gone.

After we had eaten, we picked up the cassava we had dug and gathered their leaves and tied them in a large bundle for our trip back to the village. Just before we were ready to leave, we played our familiar game.

Zena buried a cassava root as I looked away, then I searched for newly disturbed dirt to find it, but that was not easy, because we had made many holes. After it had taken me a long time of trying to find it, she called out, "close" or "not close" to help me, but sometimes she didn't tell me the truth until I begged and became angry. There were times when I got too close and nearly found it, which brought Zena running to push me away. We shoved and locked arms, testing each other's strength, but never hurting, always laughing.

After we had laughed so hard we began to cry, we knew there was no fun left in this day at the cassava field. On the path back to the monkey bridge, I remembered what I had done.

"Ouch, ouch," I said, crying as if I had stepped on something sharp. My bundle of cassava greens fell to the ground. I started to hop like a frog but on just one leg.

"Sit and me see." Zena reached and pulled her heavy bundle of cassava roots to the ground as she squatted as if going pee.

I showed her my foot. I tried my best to cry without really needing to, but no tears came. She inspected my foot and rubbed her hand over it, soft at first then harder when I could not tell her the same spot where it hurt. Finally, she let go of my foot, put her bundle on her head, then walked away in silence. I stopped my empty crying. I picked up my load and followed. I began to worry that Zena would become angry and tell Father what I had done to the bridge.

We arrived at the river. Zena seemed lost. "Where's bridge? The path here…no bridge." Zena removed the bundle from her head and set it on the ground. She looked up and down the river. Then she turned quickly and looked at me. Her eyes were wide circles, white fried eggs with a black yoke.

I shifted my head to the side and allowed the bundle of cassava leaves to fall to the ground. I set down the water bucket and food pail beside the cassava roots. I placed my hands on my hips. "It was right there." I don't recall lying to Zena before—and it was really not a lie.

She said nothing. She knew what had happened and maybe she even understood what I didn't. She hefted her bundle to her head, picked up the other things, then walked downstream. I kept complaining that I was tired and thirsty, but Zena continued to walk, ignoring me.

We took many extra steps before we came to another bridge and finally got home. She didn't tell Father about the bridge; he would have beaten both of us.

Not long after I had cut the monkey bridge and still during my eighth rice field, I heard Zena leave her room. I rose from the corner where I slept. Zena and Grandma Crowcoco, whose white hair collected the silver light from the full moon, walked together toward the center of the village. I followed them. Zena noticed me but said nothing.

Zena and Grandma Crowcoco joined some other women who were already on their knees praying to the moon. I knelt next to Zena. This reminded me of the Society and how Zena and I had prayed for the devil to stop eating the girls.

I whispered to Zena. "What are we praying for?" I leaned forward. The moon shone on Zena's shiny face. Small beads of oil had risen to the surface of her skin and made tiny moons. She seemed different, half asleep and half awake. "It didn't work to save those girls," I said. She was mumbling and gazing above. "Zena?" She just stared above. "Zena?"

"It saved you," she said, without breaking her focus on the moon.

I paused and considered that, then said, "The Society is not fair to hurt young girls."

"The young forget."

"This isn't true."

Zena's head rotated to the left as if she had the neck of an owl. Her eyes were open, alert, and blinked once. "Quiet." Her neck moved her face back to the moon.

"I remember everything. How could I forget the devil, and when I close my eyes and try to sleep, I hear the noise of them cutting me, and I think I hear the bell and the sound the switch makes, whipping through the air. Zena, I will never forget."

"Go to the hut!"

I left them and watched from Zena's bedroom window as they prayed to the moon. Perhaps Zena and Grandma Crowcoco were praying for me, because I felt a warm and deep sense of peace in my chest. The fine hairs on my arms stood, and my skin became rough as if it were the skin of a plucked chicken. I wondered if a moon devil would appear as the Society Devil had. I rested my chin on my hands and continued to watch, but my eyes wanted to close.

Even at the time, I doubted I would forget what had happened at the Society, and I never have. After the Society, my anger toward my father reached a new plateau of hatred that was miles above where it had last stood. I did not blame the Society.

It was cause and effect, between me scalding my father and him sending me to the Society to have my womanhood removed. Perhaps he would have spared me, if I had been a good daughter.

When I recorded this part of my story, I wept into the microphone. I repeated, "I was a bad daughter," and cried harder. I don't remember how long I cried, but it was a desperate cry, one that had been swallowed for more than fifty years and was finally let go.

Once I was cried-out and I had apologized over and over and over, I was gently reminded of what most of us know—children of abuse tend to blame themselves. I had wanted to forget, like Zena said she had, but I remember that horrible night. Perhaps she was telling the truth. She had forgotten. I suspect for her, this centuries-old custom was the norm for all girls her age, a rite of passage. She had not internalized the loss of her womanhood as punishment. I had.

# 13
# The Devil Ate Mama Kama

The new sun was bright and hot on my face. I began to wake. I was in Zena's bed, thinking my arms were wrapped around her neck, because I smelled the oil that gathered on her face at night, but it was only the oils that had wiped on the fabric of her pillowcase. I squeezed to make sure and felt and heard the familiar crunching of the dried palm fronds that filled her pillow.

I sprang off the bed and peered out the window, looking for the Moon Devil. The Moon Devil hadn't come last night, at least for as long as I had watched Zena and Grandma Crowcoco. They were not there on their knees where I had last seen them. I searched the hut. Father was also gone. I went to Mama Kama's room. The door had been left open. Zena was not there, so I looked through the window of Mama Kama's room, which faced the path that led to the river. No one was in sight.

I turned to leave but saw something strange sticking out from behind the door. Zena and I had hidden behind this same door when we played hide and seek. The thing sticking out from behind the door appeared to be a brown bone, maybe a finger bone, a long one that might have been stolen from a grave.

The skinless finger pointed toward the window. I turned my head slowly, not wanting to take my eyes from the finger too soon. I took a quick glance to see what the finger wanted me to see. Nothing. I drew a deep breath, let it out, then moved closer to the door to get a better look at the finger.

"Zena? Why are you hiding in Mama Kama's room?" No answer came. "Zena, what is that you're holding. It looks like...a dead man's finger." Leaning back, I stretched my leg and hooked the edge of the door with my toe. I pulled slowly, ready to run and jump out the window.

The finger turned into a boney hand. Then a cool morning gust came from the window, the door slammed closed. The most scary thing appeared!

"Haaaaa!"

It was the Society Devil! I screamed, unable to move. Pee ran down my stiff legs.

"Help! Zena!"

I trembled. My head shook, violently, back and forth so fast that my vision became blurry.

"But...but...its body is flat," I said to myself. And...and...its head was not on top of its shoulders, but it was hanging upside down on its chest—more frightening than ever!

"Jabonkah! You peed on my floor!"

I jumped back and ran toward Mama Kama's voice. She was leaning inside through her window.

"Why are you in here?" She ran around the hut and hurried into her room, pushing the door open, shoving the Society Devil against the wall again.

I grabbed her fat leg. "The Society Devil is behind your door!"

She pulled me off and said, "Wait outside my room."

I ran from her and she slammed the door. I listened for the fight between the Society Devil and Mama Kama. While I waited, I wiped the pee from the insides of my legs with my hands and rubbed them together until they were dry. I heard movement but not the sounds of a fight.

"Are...you okay...Mama Kama?" I wondered what I would do if I heard the Society Devil crunching Mama Kama's bones but then thought that because her legs and arms were so fat I might not hear the cracking of bones for a long time. I lay on my stomach and peeked under the door, thinking I might see a puddle of red blood and bits of black flesh.

Her door burst open, almost hitting me in the head. The Society Devil jumped from Mama Kama's bedroom! I sprang up and screamed and screamed and screamed, then cried, "Zena, help!" I tried to run, but the Society Devil grabbed my arms. "Zena!"

The Society Devil began to laugh, as I yanked and tried to wiggle free. "Child stop...stop before you hurt yourself." It was Mama Kama's voice. The Society Devil sounded just like Mama Kama!

Then the most amazing devil-magic happened. The Society Devil raised its arms and its boney fingers and broke off its own horrifying head. The light in my mind dimmed. My eyes must have rolled in circles as the room began to spin. I fell to my knees with my nose shoved to the ground.

"Look at me."

"No, Devil. Leave Mama Kama alone!" I didn't want to see a headless devil, but it squeezed my arm till it hurt. I looked up. "Aaaah, aaaah, aaaah, *Zena!*" I screamed, letting all the noise I had in me out. The Society Devil had taken Mama Kama's head as its own.

I jumped up and began to hit the devil in the chest. I yelled, "Give Mama Kama her head back."

Mama Kama's head laughed. The Society Devil let go of my arms. Then it began to peel off its skin to reveal Mama Kama's fat body. I looked down again. I knew I was about to die.

"You may look at the devil, Jabonkah. You're a graduate of the Society." Mama Kama had never been mean to me or lied to me, so I looked.

"It's a special dress I wear during the Society."

I stood shaking. My mind stretched to understand, wider than a snake's mouth that was trying to swallow a hut. My own eyes showed me the truth, amazing as it was—I had been living with two devils, Mama Kama and Father.

I ran, searching for Zena.

# 14
# Who Cut Me?

I ran to find Zena to tell her how I had thought that the Society Devil had eaten Mama Kama, but then discovered that the Society Devil *was* Mama Kama. I passed Father's rice hut, which was full, and didn't stop to smell its flowery odor. I took the path to the river, where Zena might be fishing or washing Father's clothes. The sun was hot on my back. With each long step, I came down on my toes then up with my knees, like when I dance and I go nowhere, but now I was moving fast.

The parrots above me in the treetops squawked and flapped their wings, just the same as if I were a hawk coming for their young. I wished I were the child of a parrot. I didn't think they would hurt their young or lie to them about what was special.

I dropped from my toes and to my flat feet, slowing as I approached a swarm of bees that buzzed in a tree to the left of me. Some were walking on the ground, maybe gathering mud to make a new nest. Once I was certain I had not angered them, I ran again, rising to my toes.

The river was near. It was a constant source of life, even in the dry season. The shallow water kept the surrounding plants and trees green, the bugs fat, and the birds happy because they still had big bugs to eat.

Zena knelt in the shade at the edge of a calm pool of water. Her back was to me. She was probably scrubbing one of Father's white shirts, as I had seen her do so many times, working the suds into the collar with her thumb and rubbing the insides of the collar together.

Grandma Crowcoco stopped smacking her wound-up, red-and-blue dress on a flat rock. She stood straight. Her empty breasts hung flat against her chest. She looked at me, sensing, I thought, that I was upset.

"Jabonkah has something to say," Grandma Crowcoco said.

Zena straightened and turned. She had tied her dress above her knees to keep it dry. One of Father's shirts was in her right hand. She swiped her left arm across her forehead. "What? Are you hungry?" She sounded tired, perhaps exhausted from praying to the Moon Devil for most of the night.

I was hungry but shook my head.

"John Henry wants me?"

I stood silently, rubbing the smoothness of the mud but not burrowing my toes.

"I think she has swallowed a snake, and it needs to come out," Grandma Crowcoco said.

Grandma Crowcoco always said impossible things that usually made me laugh but not this time.

"A new game, Jabonkah?" Zena said.

Grandma Crowcoco grinned. "As I said, the poor girl swallowed a snake, and it has eaten her words." Grandma Crowcoco let out a big laugh. "Finally, we will have rest from all of her words, Zena."

Zena turned away, squatted, then shoved Father's shirt under the reddish brown water. She twisted it into a cord, squeezed out the water, and shook it out. She moved to her left and dunked it over and over and over into a bucket of rainwater, which we saved just for his white shirts.

"Jabonkah, you out of words?" Zena finally said, looking up from her wash.

Zena. The only person I loved and cared about was making fun of me. Yes, we had teased each other when we were playing but not when I was obviously upset.

Grandma Crowcoco bent and began hitting the dress again. "Maybe the devil took her—"

"Mama Kama is the devil!" I shouted, as if this were the deepest secret in Bomi Hills. "I wanted to, but I was afraid to ask if she had cut me." My bottom lip began to quiver. I sucked it in to hold it still.

Zena came out from the river. Copper-colored mud clung to the tops of her toes. She opened her arms wide, but I didn't move.

"A mother not know who cuts daughter," Zena said.

I jumped so hard into her that Zena had to take a step back. My tears let go like a dark cloud releases its rain. Zena pulled my head and put her cool hands on my face. She rubbed me with soothing tenderness. I reached with my left hand and patted the top of her head. It was warm and wet with sweat.

"Those related to the new graduates don't help during that part of the Society," Grandma Crowcoco said, then added, "Zena had asked me the same question."

I had not considered that. I pulled away from Zena. "Why do we do this to each other? I can still feel—" Young boys ran past us and jumped into the water to our left, downstream. "Why can they," I pushed back from Zena and pointed to the boys, "come to the river before girls who are the same number of rice fields? And, don't tell me it's a man's world. Those are boys."

Both Zena and Grandma Crowcoco stared at me in the strangest way. Their foreheads wrinkled and their mouths came partly open. Then they looked at my outstretched left arm. I was pointing at the boys. "Where she get these words?" Zena said to Grandma Crowcoco.

Grandma Crowcoco said nothing. She moved her eyes from my left arm to Zena's eyes.

"I am not a witch!" I turned and ran, feeling a deep sadness growing within me. More boys passed me. I hated them.

I ran into the rice hut without remembering how I had gotten there and climbed the bundles, smelling my favorite thing but not enjoying its fragrance. At the top, near the metal roof, the heat was so strong that my body prickled in bumps, and a chill ran through me from the ends of my toes to the tips of my ears.

My separation from Zena grieved me, and my differences from others had never been so apparent. I bit the skin between my thumb and the first finger of my left hand, wanting to bite a hole. My chest heaved as my body began to heat up. Sweat beaded on my forehead and temples.

"This is my world," I said in a growl, my teeth still biting down on my skin. "I'll rule my world. I'll decide what is special," I said with another growl. I bit harder, feeling more pain, daring myself to join my teeth together.

A whimper jumped out of my chest just as I thought I could bite through. I dropped my hand from my mouth and lay my head against an itchy bundle of rice stalks. The hot air burned the inside of my nose, but I endured the burn, so I could smell the beautiful, clean rice.

I remembered how I had driven the birds when they just wanted food. They did what was natural for them—eat the rice. *Why was everyone trying to drive me away from who I was?* I thought, just before the dryness in my nose made me sneeze.

Zena loved me. She told me I was different, but she had always accepted what was natural for me even if it had meant a beating for her.

I consider now, as an adult, that Zena may have satisfied, through me, her desires to rebel against "the man rules" or, and I laugh whenever I think this, that Zena may have simply lived in a constant state of amazement of my strange words and notions.

I looked at my skin to see if I were roasting like a chicken over a fire or drying out like a fish in the sun. I climbed down and ran to our hut.

Zena was rubbing the wrinkles out of father's shirt with a smooth stone.

"Zena?"

She turned.

I wrapped my arms around her and squeezed her chest, placing my head under her chin. "Does Father want to drive me off?" Zena stroked my hair. "Was he hoping that the devil would eat me like it did the other girls?"

Zena kissed the top of my head.

"Why does he hate me and beat you, Zena?"

"Man rules."

"But why?"

She began to rock us both back and forth, as if comforting a baby. "John Henry says you to go to school."

I shook my head. "No, I will not stay if he takes me."

"The rain over, so you go."

"I am a bush woman like you. That's all I want. I will always be with you. I am already learning so much, and, for the next rice field, I will cut the rice like you. I can help you more and fish with you and Grandma Crowcoco, and I can already dig cassava, and climb the banana tree without getting hurt, and make fires, and everything you do but…be with Father. How can you stand that?" I paused for a breath. "And, I was sold to a man. When will he come and get me? I don't want a man. Who would?"

"John Henry decide. You go."

I let go of her, took her hands; they smelled of soap, the Lava soap the missionaries brought to us. "But I will not stay."

"He will beat you."

I drew Zena's thumb into my mouth and pretended to eat it. I mumbled, "I'm hungry."

Zena laughed, then freed her thumb. "You go to market." She squeezed my cheeks together, turning my lips round. "But come back fast. I cook for John Henry and you."

# 15
# Palm Oil and Salt

Constant rain turned the long road from our village to Bomi Hills into gooey mud, which was not a problem for me, but it was for Father. He came home less often during the rainy season. He lived in his Bomi Hills kingdom, I assumed, and he could not force me to go to school if he were not at home. But the rainy season was over and that meant Father would walk the long, dry roads back to our village on more days than he would stay in Bomi Hills.

I didn't know at that young age, nor now, why my father preferred to live as a tribal man in our village when he could have spent most of his time in the more civilized Bomi Hills. I suspect that in Bomi Hills, the presence of the white men he worked with prevented him from ruling as he could and did in our village, where he was a king. He reined over our entire village not just his household.

After the rains stopped, I heard the great noises from a diesel engine, and I knew Father would return to our village more often because the roads were dry. He would force me to go to school.

A big, yellow machine shook the ground and sent streams of grey smoke into the blue sky. Churning metal ribbons made horrible squeaking noises. They spun black wheels around that made me dizzy to watch. A red fog rose out of the dirt and filled the air. The ground tumbled and rolled in the mouth of the giant, silver blade. The machine drove the red earth toward the middle of the road, where great chunks filled the deep splits that angry waters had torn. The machine left smaller ruts on the sides of the road where I walked and watched this magical event.

Once the road was flat, the big, yellow machine and the noise and the smoke left, but a dirty red mist stayed, coating the trees and bushes along the edges of the road, making their bright-green leaves dull and sad looking.

I held a quarter in my hand, walking in the small ruts. When the road had deep ruts, the animals that lived on the ground and in the bushes were easier to see. I didn't have to bend over far to see them. Now I had to almost crawl to find my friends.

I saw the blackest blood oozing from under a brown banana leaf. I thought the earth was hurt. I lifted the leaf with a stick and found a small red snake with a large yellow and green frog in its mouth. Instinctively, I opened my mouth to help the snake swallow the frog.

I noticed the frog's unhappy face and felt sad for her and her baby frogs, until it occurred to me that the frog might be the mean father of baby frogs. Then I became happy for the snake and let the leaf down on the snake and his meal.

Still bent over, I walked slowly and soon spotted a young, gray rabbit nibbling at the tender roots of a seedling palm tree. It occurred to me that if the rabbit didn't eat the young palms, there would be more trees with coconut milk to drink. But then the men in my village and my father would just make more palm wine and be drunk all the time and force the women and children to work harder. I scratched my head and thought that we might have more oil if the rabbits didn't eat the toes of baby palm trees.

"Palm oil and salt," I said to myself. Father would want to eat as soon as he got home, so it was important to have his food ready, or he might beat Zena, and this made me worry, because sometimes I forgot what Zena needed from the store.

Often I had to make several trips back to Zena before I got the right things. Zena usually sent me earlier in the day, knowing I needed at least one reminder trip and sometimes two before I got what she wanted. While it was true that I was easily distracted by what I saw on the way to the store, I was especially forgetful when I talked to the children and adults I met on the way.

"Hi, Jabonkah!" It was mean Martha and her sister, who lived in a house on the road to the Bomi Hills market. They wore dresses like Zena and Grandma Crowcoco. I still just had a cloth for my front.

I ran up to them and inspected their colorful dresses and hats. "My Christmas dress is prettier. It covers my feet and comes to my wrists. Is your dress from an older sister or cousin? I don't have an older sister, so I am the only one to wear my dress." My smile must have been big. I was always happy to talk about my Christmas dress.

They laughed. "Maybe you should wear it," Martha said. Then she put her hands on my shoulders and turned me around. "Because your butt is showing." She shoved me. I stumbled but didn't fall. "Can't your father buy you a wrap that goes all the way around your waist?" Both sisters laughed.

I jerked back, facing them. "My father is John Henry, and he owns the biggest rice field and hugest rice hut and works at the mine and dresses in a white shirt every day."

"How many wives does he have?" They stared at me, their hands on their hips.

"He has three wives," I said, then quickly added with great pride, "He is building a kingdom."

Martha's two little brothers came out of the house. Both were taller than me, but I was older than the oldest boy by at least two rice fields. I stepped up on a mound of dried mud, but the boys were still taller.

"Do you know what a kingdom is?" Martha said. She wore a blue hat.

"Can you spell it?" The other sister said. She was maybe ten rice fields and wore a white-and-red hat.

"I don't go to school," I said and stuck out my chest. "I'm a bush woman like Zena. Why do I need to spell it when I can fish and make fire and drive the birds?"

"I can drive birds," said one of the brothers, who had no shirt on, like me, and wore pants that had holes in them.

"Shut up," Martha said to her brother.

Then both brothers sat on the ground with their legs crossed and stared up at me.

"Where are you going?" Martha said.

"To the market. Do *you* get to go to the market? I get to go by myself now. Zena said I can even go by myself to sell bananas when they are ripe. Can *you* climb a banana tree? I can. Look that's how I got these scars." I opened the insides of my arms and lifted them up to Martha's face.

Martha looked. "I don't see anything." The two boys on the ground jumped up and pointed to the scars that grew back lighter than the rest of my skin. They looked at Martha with faces that seemed to question her eyesight.

"Go in the hut!" Martha yelled at them. The brothers didn't move until she stomped her foot, then they ran.

She gazed at me with eyes pinched almost closed. "What are you buying at the store, Jabonkah?"

I scratched the top of my left foot with the bottom of my right. "Palm oil and…" I had forgotten the second item. Zena never gave me more than two things to buy. I had to say something. "And a canned chicken," bubbled out of my mouth.

"Canned chicken?" Both girls laughed and the two brothers also, who were draped over the window watching. Martha said, "Why would you buy a canned chicken when your father has so many live chickens you could eat?"

I was hungry for chicken, so that could have been the reason I'd said that. "Maybe it…was sugar…or coffee."

"Or, maybe, you're a stupid bush woman like your mother."

I jumped at Martha and choked her, then I quickly became aware of how big her neck was compared to my small hands. I was amazed at how strong Martha was to lift me so high and toss me so far. I landed on my back on the mound I had been standing on.

My breath jumped out of me and would not come back in. I stood. I tried to breathe but only a wheeze came in. I shifted to my hands and knees, looking up at the sisters who were now in the house, hovering out the same window with the two boys.

Half hurt feelings and half back pain combined to make me breathless until, finally, small sharp gasps returned. My quarter? I stood and looked in my left hand then my right—nothing. The youngest boy must have understood that I had lost my quarter. He ran from the house, retrieved my coin, then handed it to me. He went back in the house.

As I turned to go back to Zena, for her to remind me of the second item,

Martha's words thundered inside my whole body: "You're a stupid bush woman." I repeated this over and over and over in my head, moving quickly on the shaved part of the road and not in the small ruts to look for animals. I held the quarter in my hand, wishing to remember what Zena needed from the market. Zena was the best bush woman, and I wanted to be like her. "Those girls could not do half of what Zena and I can," I grumbled in anger.

I let the sweat from my forehead enter my eyes and sting them. I didn't want to break my rhythm to wipe it away. "Salt!" my mind shouted at me. "Palm oil and salt." I thought about turning around, but I was already at my village. I would run back to the market, after I hugged Zena, and not stop to talk to anyone who might try to trick me.

Zena stood outside, waiting for me. She must have seen me coming.

"Did you forget again?" Her eyes opened in a warm and gentle way.

"Yes, Zena. Those girls made me forget. But then I remembered again on my way back to you, but I kept coming because I needed you." I paused for a shallow breath. It hurt to breathe any deeper. "Those girls said mean things to me."

She pulled me into her arms. I entered. She held me tight.

"Palm oil and salt, right?"

"Yes, but you tried to go back?"

"No, I must go or Father will be angry." I stood on my toes and kissed both of her dimples. I ran as fast as I could and repeated, "Palm oil and salt," with each step, staying out of the ruts, ignoring the two sisters who called my name and yelled, "Palm oil and sugar, vinegar, coffee." I yelled to myself, over and over, "Palm oil and salt," as if these were the only words I knew.

I got to the market, stepped inside on its splintery wood, and I continued to whisper, "Palm oil and salt. Palm oil and salt. Palm oil and salt," until it was my turn at the counter. "Palm oil and salt," I said proudly.

The wrinkled Lebanese woman said, "Are you certain, Jabonkah? You know how forgetful you are." Her head tilted to the side and she smiled, showing me her golden teeth. I wondered if she had been born with teeth like that or if she had bought them in Monrovia. Perhaps Grandma Crowcoco should have yellow teeth, so she could bite a cucumber when we worked in the rice field.

"Jabonkah?"

"Yes."

"What does Zena want?" Her smile was gone.

"Palm oil and sugar."

"Are you certain, Jabonkah, not salt or coffee for John Henry?" She wiped her hands on her green apron.

I rubbed my forehead as it itched from the coating of dust and sweat. I looked at the canned chicken on the shelf and almost said that but remembered what Martha had said about having so many live ones. I began to get this feeling inside, like someone was digging a hole in me, making me feel empty but at the same time filling me with doubt. I stared at the picture on the canned chicken. My mouth began to water. I swallowed and licked my lips. Salt! I tasted salt!

"Zena wants palm oil and *salt!*" I remembered! I jumped up and down like a monkey with a banana in each hand.

"Fine, palm oil and salt it is. Now, did you remember to bring money?"

I opened my left hand and showed her my quarter. It was covered in dirt. She made a hissing sound with her mouth and shook her head. I rubbed the mud off on my wrap and offered it to her again. She looked at my right side. I switched the quarter to my right hand. She took it.

# 16
# Beggars

Because my father worked for the Liberian Mining Company in Bomi Hills and because he owned one of the largest rice fields and rice huts, he could afford to send me to school. Other men from the surrounding villages, who also worked for the Liberian Mining Company, paid for their children to get an education.

Zena had never gone to school, and she was the best bush woman in the whole Gola Tribe. Although I hadn't met every one of them, I was certain she was better than all the others. Father never complained about Zena, except when he thought she had been with other men. Maybe she was also the best at other things, which I didn't care to think about, but it was something Father liked about her that made him not want to share. I am certain that he didn't care if Mama Kama had been with other men. She was old and fat. I didn't even like looking at her.

All I wanted was to be left alone so I could be just like Zena—well, not when it came to that thing she had to do with Father—and if she never went school, then neither would I, unless Father forced me.

I loved the rain, a falling river, where opportunities to play were just outside the entrance to our hut. And, best of all, the heavy rains had meant no school. I didn't have a pair of shoes, but the sticks and rocks that the gooey mud hid were not a problem for me, because my feet were hard and rough like the bottom of a dog's paw. So I could have gone to school, but the man ruled less when he was not home.

Father hated to walk home in the mud, so he would not come home from work during the worst rains. He stayed in Bomi Hills, in another part of his kingdom, for weeks at a time. Because he always wore his black shoes, his feet were softer than those of the other men of our tribe, so that kept him from walking the long distances on the muddy roads.

Some rain came with flashes of lightning and thunder that seemed to roll over the tops of trees like waves on the shore. Zena made me come inside if the spears of light fell from the sky. She told me God spoke to us with his thunder, and he made the light to find the people who had angered him. Zena and I hid in her room. God was speaking and looking for those he wanted to punish. He was, according to the missionaries who brought soap, another man, after all, who wanted to rule.

Zena and I were under her bed during one storm, which came with lots of lightning. I said to her, "Does Father stay outside when God is speaking?" She didn't answer but squeezed me tighter. Just then, a flash of light drove away all the darkness, even from under the bed, showing me Zena's big smile. So I smiled too.

Life was better without a man to rule, but now the heavy rains had stopped, and Zena made me practice extending my right hand to Father when he approached our village. He would give us money if I held out my right hand, but he would beat me if I offered him my left hand.

We needed this money to buy the things we couldn't grow ourselves. He gave us money so we could buy things for his food, not ours. I would have eaten rice and cassava for the rest of my life if it meant not having to ask him for money. But he expected us to ask so we could buy the things he wanted, and if he didn't get them, he beat Zena.

Training to be right handed began once again. Zena stood in the entrance of the hut. It was raining, but these were not the heavy rains of winter. She made me run from the rice hut to her. As I ran, I slapped my right hand against my leg to remind myself to offer her that one, not the left hand. I stopped in front of Zena, took a quick breath, then offered my right hand. It seemed too easy. Zena looked puzzled.

"Hug legs next time. Try again."

"Why? He never hugs me."

She grasped my right hand and pushed down my arm. "Hug him first. You look like beggar."

I stomped my foot. "We *are* beggars. I would rather go hungry."

Zena's eyes closed off to mine, acting as if I had cut a second monkey bridge. "Try again."

I walked in the rain toward the rice hut, splashing my feet into the bottoms of the puddles, while making deep grunting sounds in my throat, like Grandpa when he squats behind his hut to poo.

I turned. Zena waited. I waited. She waved for me to come. I ran, jumping over the puddles, determined I would succeed. I slid into Zena. I hugged her middle as if they were Father's tall legs. I may have held too long because it was Zena and not Father. I let go of her and opened my right hand, begging for money. We practiced until I had soaked Zena's dress, and she was shivering.

Our beggar's training continued for several days. Zena and I took turns watching for Father's tall figure coming down the road. On the day we saw him coming, the sky was deep blue. The leaves on the trees shone green, like they had been freshly painted.

Zena thought this might be the day Father would come home. She helped me bring dry wood, which we kept in the rice hut during the rains, and I started the fire, with a little help from Zena. She knew where the smoke needed her breath. She blew on it gently until yellow flames danced.

She cooked cassava flour to make dumboy, then boiled its leaves in the same water. I scooped a handful of rice kernels from a bag, brought it to the mortar, then dumped it in. I began to pound the rice as Zena had taught me.

I was confident I would get quarters from Father, especially after Zena and I had practiced for many days. I hummed along with Zena, happy she made more dumboy than Father could eat and happy I was going to make her proud of me.

I finished pounding the rice in the mortar. I scooped handfuls, first blowing away the worst of the chaff, then dumped the grain onto the winnowing tray. The red sun warmed the cool winds that drove the white clouds apart. I tossed the rice in the breeze, which caught each curved piece of chaff and made it fly, like the kites the children who live in Bomi Hills have.

Zena finished boiling the cassava leaves. She wanted me to put the rice in the same water but didn't allow me to pour all of the rice in. She knew how much rice was needed to prevent it from being too watery or uncooked in the center, something I had yet to learn.

Once we were done cooking, I swept the biggest pieces of dried mud from our hut and out the entrance. Zena prepared the table for Father. It was one of the largest amounts of food I remembered having: a mound of rice Zena topped with small bits of wild onion; a folded banana leaf that held steamed, dried fish with hot peppers inside, which she had roasted on the coals and I'd had to flip many times; and potatoes she fried in the last of our palm oil. Over a bowl of cut fruit, Zena squeezed lemon juice to keep the butter pears and bananas from turning brown.

"There he is!" I cried. I jumped up and down, shaking my hands as if they were wet and I wanted them dry. "Zena, I will forget, and you will not get the money!"

"Not forget." She waved her arms and hands up and down to cool me as when I had a fever. She picked something off my nose, maybe a piece of chaff, then took my right hand and bit my thumb.

"Ouch!" I yanked it from her mouth, ripping it across her sharp teeth.

"Now, you remember. Go!"

I ran to his tall, dark figure. I wanted to suck on my sore thumb, but as I ran, I needed to use my elbows to pump up and down, as if running away from Mamma Kama, the Society Devil. The sun felt hot on my back. My stomach growled, reminding me of the food we had made for Father and leftovers that I would have to eat if he didn't eat it all.

I got close to Father, slowed, stopped, then stood still. He reached into his pocket then pulled his hand out. I noticed his shoes were covered with mud. I wrapped my arms around his legs. Feelings of affection surprised me for the man who never smiled and never said good words to me, unless he was at work with the white men.

My face rested between his knees. I waited for a return hug, but Father plucked me away like I was a twig of cockleburs that clung to his trousers. I looked into his fierce eyes. My feelings of love disappeared. Feelings of hatred returned.

He extended his right arm and opened his hand, exposing two silver quarters. Just as quickly as I had reached for them, he made a fist and struck me on the top of my head.

My legs weakened. I fell cross-legged, seeing blackness. He walked past me. I started to cry. I remembered the pain in my right thumb. Zena would get the belt. I rubbed the top of my head and wailed. I was not aware of the length of time I sat in the road, crying, but I stopped my feelings of selfpity when Father began yelling at Zena.

"None, John Henry," Zena said.

I ran toward our hut calling out, "Zena! Zena!" repeatedly, feeling a burning in my throat as if my heart were climbing out. I stopped in the doorway to Zena's room. Father had tied her arms to the posts of the bed. He had his belt in his hand. I moved to the side. Zena had many welts on her back the size of the buckle.

"You are lying! I can smell them. How many men were here!"

Zena cringed forward, anticipating the next strike. "None, none, please, please don't, please."

Her voice was so sad. I cried out, "Stop it!" I grabbed Father's legs as he swung the belt over his head and gave Zena another blow. I jumped on his back. The sound of the thud and Zena's moan had unleashed a rage in me.

Father yelled, "Get off me, witch." He grabbed my arms and hurled me against the wall. I lay in a heap, tears blurring my vision. The thuds of the buckle made hollow drum sounds as they struck Zena.

"Zena! Zena!" I cried over and over.

The drumming continued. Father called her horrible names and accused her of being with more men than there were in our village.

The beating stopped.

His shadow came close to me. He kicked my thigh. He left the room, slamming the door. I leaped to Zena. Her back was bloody and ripped apart. If a panther had clawed her, it would look the same.

As I untied Zena, I said, "Oh, Zena, why, why?" Her face was wet with tears but she made no sounds of crying. She folded over. I jumped onto the bed. I kissed her face then pulled on her arms. The ends of her legs drooped off the mattress.

Wishing to kill my father, I grunted while I pulled her onto the bed. Looking at her back made my stomach sick. Flies with blue-green bodies must have smelled the blood. More and more came to land on her. I kept driving them away, while I laid Zena's oldest dress gently across her.

On the bed next to her, I curled around her and stroked her face. "Zena, Mommy, you'll be okay."

Last time Father had beat her like this, I had scalded him, hoping he would die. I knew of no other means to stop his ruling other than to cut his head off with a machete, or maybe I would remove his arms. Then he could not beat Zena or me.

# 17
# School

Once the roads had dried, Father came home frequently. I wished the rains could continue forever if it meant he would never return. Zena moved slowly. She lifted the rice pot, causing her face to twist in a sour way. Her wounds were healing from the last beating Father had given her, but her bones on the side of her chest still hurt when she lifted heavy things or breathed in deeply.

My cheek had swollen from the angry blow of his hand, but my spirit could no longer be bruised by his hand or buckle. I hated my father, this man's world, where he ruled over me and Zena.

He didn't want me to become a bush woman like Zena. I complained that Zena needed help, but he demanded I attend school, and, not wishing more trouble for Zena, I let him to take me to school on his way to work. I gave him no resistance while we walked to school, at least not enough to cause him to jerk his belt from his pants and beat me.

I tried to stay close to Father. I had quickly learned that walking too far behind would make him angry. He knew if I saw him remove his belt, I would run, so he would slip it off when I was not looking. Then when I got close, he would hit me wherever the buckle would fall on my body. Now, if I got distracted, all he had to do was call my name and place his hands on his belt, and I would run to get close to him.

Walking next to Father, I tried very hard not to talk to the monkeys or smell the flowers that called to me. Father's legs were long, and at times I had to run to keep up.

"Hi, Jabonkah!" It was one of Martha's younger brothers. "Where're you going?"

"To school. Why else would I carry my lunch?" I said, annoyed he would talk to me when I was upset. I lifted my silver can, which Zena had made special for me, by the string so he could see. The can contained rice and dried fish that was covered with cassava greens.

The boy said, "I already know my ABCs!"

I stuck my tongue out at him and ran to get closer to Father. I sort of knew the ABCs. I just didn't know their order. Zena didn't need to know them to be a bush woman, so neither did I.

"Jabonkah!" Father held his hand on his belt. I clutched my lunch can tightly and ran. When I got close to him, he struck me with his knuckles. The leaves on the trees and bushes twirled in a blur of green. The white clouds and blue sky tipped upside-down then up again, rocking back and forth, making me nauseous. My knees weakened and caused me to sit. I closed my eyes.

My fish and cassava greens spilled on the ground, so I began to cry. Father pulled on my arm. I reached for and caught the string of my lunch can. The ground had my cassava leaves and dried fish, but I had my rice.

"Stop crying!" Father demanded. I did. He dragged me while I attempted to walk, and he didn't let go until we arrived at school.

The long school hut had a big room with a concrete floor. The teacher sat at a desk in the front. A blackboard with dusty white swirls hung on the wall behind her.

I stood next to Father, closer to his legs than normal. The children stared, looking at me from my head to my toes. They leaned next to each other and whispered and laughed just as quietly. Some were pointing at me.

Father spoke to the teacher, who had stood when she saw us enter, but I didn't listen. I recognized Martha and her sister. They must have been making comments about my dimples. They pointed at me, then they poked their index fingers into their cheeks, until their lips made a puffy circle, like the butt of a monkey.

I stuck out my tongue at Martha, but many of the children stuck out their tongues at me. I didn't care. I was not going to be here for long. After Father disappeared down the road, I would run back to Zena.

Father placed his hand on my head, twisting my body, forcing me to face the teacher. I sucked my tongue in my mouth. She offered her pink palm, which I must have looked at for too long, because Father knocked me on the head with his fist as if it were a coconut.

I slipped my dirt-crusted hand into hers, which was soft and smooth like Zena's breasts. She bent in half and smiled at me. I looked down at her brown-leather sandals. Her toenails were all cut to the same length and painted pink, like her fingernails.

"My name is Miss Johnson. What is yours, young lady?"

Her words were as gentle as her hand. I looked up but avoided a direct gaze. Her brown skin had no bumps or wrinkles. Her lips smiled. My lips parted with hers, showing my teeth like she was showing me, white, straight, and even, like none I had seen before.

Father bumped his leg into me. "Tell her your name."

Her eyes reminded me of Zena's—loving. "Jabonkah Sackey," I said softly. Father pinched my ear and twisted it. I yelled, "Jabonkah Sackey."

The children laughed.

"Quiet, please," Miss Johnson said. She pulled me away from Father and held my hand. I felt like a fish she had caught that she didn't want to slip away. She made me face the class. I stuck out my tongue again. Miss Johnson must have noticed. She leaned forward, placed her long finger on the tip of my tongue, and pushed it back in my mouth.

"Children." They all sat up in their chairs and looked at her. "Please say hello to Jabonkah."

They smiled at Miss Johnson and said, "Hello, Jabonkah."

Martha folded her arms and glared at me. I wanted to show her my longer tongue, but Miss Johnson was leaning over and watching me, perhaps knowing what I might do.

She led me to a seat in the front of the others. I sat and placed my lunch can on the floor beside me. My father left without speaking, but he grabbed at his belt as he passed by. I had to stay at least for this day, or he might beat me and Zena after he got home.

All morning, I watched and listened to Miss Johnson, who reminded me of a beautiful bird with a happy song. She treated me with kindness, like I had only received from Zena and Grandma Crowcoco. Her eyes, eyebrows, and smile changed in interesting ways as she spoke. Her body was tall and slender, and she wore a dress that was not African, but it was one that hugged her thin waist. It was in two pieces: white at the top, shaping her breasts, and black at the bottom, short, showing her legs below her knees.

Later in the morning, Miss Johnson said, "Jabonkah, will you please recite your ABCs?" She waited for me to talk. I turned around in case there was another Jabonkah who knew her ABCs. She came close, bent low, and said, "Jabonkah, can you tell me your ABCs?" She paused again for me to talk.

I didn't.

"Please, try for me."

She asked so nicely that I sat up, smiled at her, and nodded eagerly. I remembered the first three letters, but when I got to "D" I said "G."

The children burst into laughter.

"Class, please," Miss Johnson said, with her eyebrows pinched together.

They stopped laughing so quickly I looked around to see if they were still there.

Miss Johnson went to her desk, took a single piece of paper from a drawer, then brought it to me. "This is the alphabet, Jabonkah. Have your mother go over this with you."

"She can't! She's a stupid bush woman, just like Jabonkah." I didn't have to turn to see who had said that. It was Martha. Filled with anger, I jumped up, but Miss Johnson grabbed my arm before I could rush to beat Martha.

"That's enough, class. There will be no more outbursts." Her face twisted. I imagined that she could have had a splinter under her fingernail—her face was that painful. The room became quiet. Right away, Miss Johnson seemed happy again. "Take your lunch now, children," she said.

A great noise thundered behind me. I sat and waited for it to stop: scooting chairs, shuffling shoes on a sandy floor, and laughter mixed with loud talking. Miss Johnson went to her desk, sat, then began to move her papers to different places on her desk.

I pinched the string, which Zena had tied through holes she had punched in the can with a rock and an old nail, and lifted my lunch can. I carried it outside and sat by the door, away from the other children who played tag or ate their lunches. Some kept looking at me. I tried not to look back at them, but I was curious why their eyes found me interesting to see. Martha stared the most.

I had been saving a glob of rubber in my cheek. Father had told me it was forbidden to chew it in school. I removed the rubber from my mouth and stuck it on the side of my lunch can. I scooted sideways, turning my back to Martha and the other children. I held my can up. I sighed. I was very hungry, and there was only rice. I had wanted to pick up my fish and cassava leaves from the road, but Father would not have allowed it.

Someone came beside me and cast a shadow. It was her—Martha. She swiped a hand for my rubber gum, but I swiped quicker and plucked it before she could, then I plopped it in my mouth. I stretched my tongue out of my mouth longer than I had ever done before, pointing it in Martha's ugly face.

She grabbed my cheeks with her thumb and first finger and tried to squeeze my mouth open. I kicked her in the chest, hitting one of her new breasts. She yelped and jumped backward.

Martha held her right breast. "Go home, you stupid bush girl."

Miss Johnson appeared and stood next to where I sat. I could not see Miss Johnson's expression, but it made Martha go away without looking at me.

After lunch, and back in the classroom, Martha had changed seats so she could sit directly behind me. When Miss Johnson turned to the blackboard, Martha flipped my ears with her fingers, whispered, "Stupid bush dog," then slapped me on the side of my head. The children giggled. Miss Johnson turned and faced the class, hushing them with a silent finger pressed to her lips. She looked at me. I looked at her, thankful for her presence.

As soon as Miss Johnson stepped toward her desk, I felt a sharp pain on the top of my shoulder. It was Martha. She had stabbed me with her ink pen. The class drew in their breaths. I wanted to fight her, but Miss Johnson glared at us. I sat up straight in my chair, wanting to beat Martha, but I knew Father would beat me if I did.

Once I was home, I told Zena all about what had happened. I sat cross-legged as she boiled bark from a tree. After it was ready, she laid hot strips over my shoulder and held it. The small hole Martha had made didn't need this much tending, but Zena must have known that the pen had made a bigger hole in my feelings.

"She said terrible things to me."

"Who, Jabonkah?"

"Martha. She's the mean older sister who lives near the road just before Father's work."

"What did you do?"

"Nothing, Zena." She knew my anger snapped easily, like a dried chicken bone. She rubbed my shoulder. Under her fingers, the moist smooth bark slipped back and forth.

Later, after I felt much better, we prepared Father's dinner.

The next day, Father took me to school again. It started all over. Martha sat behind me. She whispered mean things: "Your mother is a stupid bush woman" and "My mother said you're a witch."

At lunchtime, I sat far from the others, hoping no one would bother me, but Martha walked in my direction. A bunch of other children followed her.

She grabbed for the string of my lunch can and caught it, surprising me when she swooped it away. She dumped my rice and fish on the ground. A rage burst open, filling my entire body with burning anger.

The fight was on! I scrambled up her legs and body. She was a tree and her head a coconut I wanted to knock down. I curled my right arm around her neck and squeezed hard, like Zena choked chickens dead.

Martha tried to scream for Miss Johnson. She shook violently, and her pounding arms kept me from cutting her breath off. I squeezed with all my strength, hoping she would die. Finally, Martha got weaker. She stopped fighting, then fell to the ground with me falling on top of her. The children screamed for Miss Johnson.

I released my hold on her neck, then pounded her head with a downpour of knotted fists. Different-colored shoes and sandals surrounded me. The children yelled my name, cheering.

As I stripped away Martha's clothes, the children took them. I jumped off her after she was naked. The cheering dried up. The children gathered around Martha.

I stood with my chest stretched back, fighting tears, trying not to call out to Zena. My heart beat so rapidly I wondered if it would break through my rib bones. I looked down at my empty lunch can and began to cry; then, after a few moments, I grabbed the string and ran home.

# 18
# Father Comes Home

Zena scraped the scorched bottom of the rice pot for a little food to replace the lunch Martha had dumped at school. While I told her the horrible story about how I had beaten Martha and stripped her naked, she paused between scrapes, shook her head, then scraped faster. After I told her all I had done, and Zena had handed me a half-empty bowl of flaky rice, she stood silently. That's when I forgot about my painful day. She seemed worried that Father would take his belt to me, and I was worried for Zena, because when he beat me, he often beat her, too.

Zena began to prepare Father a big meal, in size, at least, not in variety. He had not given us extra money for the food we had to buy at the store. She seemed overly concerned about every detail. She took Father's bamboo platter outside in the sunlight, where she scrubbed it with thick white suds, removing every bit of old food.

Her hands shook while she arranged Father's meal on the platter. The flies tried to lay their eggs on his rice, and I didn't care, but Zena inspected several clean cloths and found the whitest to cover Father's food. I wanted wiggly maggots to fill his stomach and hoped they would eat his insides.

Father would check with Miss Johnson to learn if I had remained in school, as he had the day before and as he had in his past attempts to force an education into my head.

The dogs began to bark. I ran to the window. Father approached.

Zena pulled at her dress to free her legs, so she could run faster, and came to stand beside me. We both sighed. I thought about running to the rice field, but I could not leave Zena. I squatted then rose between Zena's outstretched arms and the window. She placed her hands on my shoulders then wrapped her arms around my neck. She leaned forward, placing her cheek against mine, and began to hum deep, soothing sounds that passed through her cheek bone into mine. Zena stopped humming, separated our cheeks, then turned us toward the door.

The hot afternoon sun seemed to hold Father and prevent his dark shadow from entering the hut. Finally, the sun let go of him. He lowered his head to enter. His threatening figure bounded to the center of the room.

Zena and I trembled. We knew the belt was coming.

Father stood next to us. He smelled oily and strong like Zena did after working all day in the field. His huge hand cupped the top of my small head. His warm fingers draped down the right side of my face, squeezing my temples, causing a sharp pain. He twisted my body and broke me free from Zena's hold. I was powerless. He forced me to leave her side.

With her arms stretched toward him, Zena begged. "Please, John Henry. Not do this."

"Shut up, woman!" Father yelled.

Zena became silent. I knew she would not leave me.

Father dragged me, his crushing hold still squeezing my head. My toes barely touched the floor. He brought me next to the table, then shoved my feet to stand with angry strength, planting me like a cassava root in hard soil. He slapped my face.

"John Henry—"

He spun and glared at Zena, saying nothing. Zena cowered like a scavenging dog. She slapped her hands over her mouth.

I looked back, quickly, then straight ahead again, just the way Father had left me. I waited for the sound of his belt, small claps of thunder, as the leather slapped away from around his waist. But no little thunders came.

He moved from behind me and sat in his chair. He began to eat. "Salt, woman. Never enough." Father's cheeks puffed out, full of rice and dried fish.

Zena brought him the salt jar, set it next to his platter, then backed away out of his reach.

He pinched the white grains over his food. It seemed he was sowing a field. He stuffed his mouth full of boiled cassava greens. An oily flap hung from his mouth. His lips glistened with palm oil. His pink tongue darted out and drew in the slippery greens, creating a temporary smile, causing a smiling reflection to form on my face.

His eyes shot up at me. I took a step back. "Miss Johnson told me you got into a fight." His jaw muscles flexed hard, knotted at the corners. His teeth were hammered tight.

I placed my legs together and squeezed, trying not to pee, but it ran warm down the insides of my thighs and trickled over my ankles. I could smell it. So did he.

He stretched and looked at the floor. He shook his head and returned to his food, scooping huge mouthfuls, hardly chewing, and swallowing with great gulps. "She said," he paused. A burp rumbled from deep within him, flooded up his throat, then puffed his cheeks out. He sighed. "She said the other girl started the fight."

I nodded eagerly. I knew better than to use my words; he might slap me for using too many.

He stared at me as if it were the first time he had ever seen me. His black eyes revealed nothing of what he was thinking or feeling. "Don't start fights," he finally said, "but make damn sure you finish them." He jerked his head to the side, giving me permission to leave. He dug into the shiny greens and shoved a teetering spoonful in his mouth.

Zena had crept behind and took my arm. She pulled me slowly away from the dangers of a wild boar, it seemed. I wanted to remain in my father's presence. I was feeling differently about him and wanted more of what he had just given me.

Outside, Zena and I ran. We raced, laughing. I had never laughed so fully.

# 19
# Martha's Mother

There was no school the next day, and Father left for work or to the other part of his kingdom. Shortly after he was gone, Zena asked me to get a large can of rice from the rice hut. Our hut's supply was low, which meant the next rice harvest was not far away. At least, I hoped it was not. I always kicked the bags of open rice and told the mice or rats that might be in there to get out. I kicked the bag, and, with none leaving, I rolled down the sides, exposing the clusters of rice, to fit my large can in the bag. I took a big scoop. I folded the bag closed, then I walked back to Zena.

Father had stopped selling rice to others who had run out, so we would have what we needed. I was glad Father always made sure we had rice to eat, but I still hated him.

As I walked back to Zena, my mouth told me that I was thirsty. During the rainy season, I was never thirsty nor soon after the rainy season when the occasional storms blew in from where the sun sleeps at night. These storms gave us clear water that flowed from the roofs of our hut and the rice hut and collected in large drums.

As the water spilled off the roof, I would open my mouth under the streams. I would even stick my head in the barrels, if Father was not there to see me. The first time I tried to drink with my head underwater, I choked. I was confused, because fish could drink underwater, so I should be able to. I choked many times until I realized that fish don't have noses. I pinched my nose and drank underwater just like them.

When the rains had stopped and the rainwater in the barrels was gone, we filled the empty ones with river water, which took me many trips back and forth to the river. We let the mud settled to the bottom before we used the water for cooking and drinking, unless we could not wait to make Father his food. Neither Zena nor I cared if he ate mud.

Zena had recently told me that the rice fields were drying and that Father would soon tell us we may begin the harvest. The thought of cutting rice caused my spirits to rise like a bird riding the wind.

"Jabonkah? Jabonkah! Scoop out rice." Zena butted me with her hip.

Landing from my thoughts, I reached deep in the mortar to scoop the white grains and tan chaff, while I dipped my head inside the mortar. I breathed the aroma, the next best thing to a rice harvest. I sneezed. Something tickled my nose. I sneezed again.

"Jabonkah?"

The village dogs began to bark. The hair on their backs raised in a stiff line. I had tried once to get them to raise their hair like that, but they would not do it. I even hit them with a stick, not too hard, to make them angry and to get them to raise the hair on their backs. It never worked the same as when a stranger approached our village.

They darted off in the direction of a woman and two children, barking wildly. They usually didn't bite adults, but they liked to bite children, especially strange ones, and the smaller the better.

With the woman were Martha and her sister. I didn't think the dogs would bite them because they were older and bigger. Still, I hoped they would at least bite Martha.

Zena and I stopped working and sat on our heels. We waited. Zena probably wondered why this woman from Bomi Hills had walked into the bush and to our village, but I knew why.

After I had finished beating Martha, the younger sister said her mother would come and beat my mother. Martha's mother stood a head taller and was twice as fat as Zena.

I scooted closer to Zena. "Maybe we should go inside the hut."

Zena turned toward me. Her face was as calm as the water that sat in the rain barrel. She blinked. Her eyes grew round, and she shook her head.

The dogs followed Martha's sister. The black one nipped at her heels. She grabbed a bent stick and walked backward, swinging and swishing at the snarling bitches, yelling at them to go away.

My grandfather, Zena's father, who was blind and healed many people, came from his hut and whistled. The dogs stopped, stood, then sat in the road on their hind legs, panting. Grandfather went back into his hut. I don't know if he cared that the dogs might bite the strangers, or if he had been sleeping and the barking dogs had wakened him.

Martha's mother wore a dress unlike any I had ever seen at the market in Bomi Hills. She must have bought it in Monrovia. The color was strange. It was blue but not like the blue in the sky. It was green but not like the green of new leaves.

"Zena, what color is that?" I pointed to the mother. Zena tilted her head, and she wrinkled her chin. She shrugged. They were not colors of the bush.

The three stopped in front of us. We stood. They were all taller than Zena and me.

Martha's mother pointed at Martha's face and said, "Look at her, you stupid bush woman."

Zena's eyes focused, no doubt, looking at Martha's swollen eye.

"Yes, your daughter," she pointed an accusing finger at me, "is a witch! She is left handed and…and has dimples like you, so you are a witch too!"

Martha's mother jabbed her arm at me with a finger that I would bite off if she stuck it closer to my face.

"She will never amount to anything." Then she turned and jabbed her arm and finger at Zena. "She will be a stupid bush woman like you!"

Zena stepped close to Martha's mother and shoved her, causing her to stumble backward. Martha's mother would have fallen if both Martha and her sister had not grabbed her.

"Leave us, or I beat you worse than ugly daughter." Zena stepped forward with her hands knotted into fists, ready to beat her. I was also ready for a fight.

"No you—"

Zena pulled back her arm, like she and I had both seen Father do before he hit us. Martha's mother turned and ran. Martha and her sister followed her, and the barking dogs followed them, snapping at the youngest one's heels.

# 20
# Dimples

I didn't realize it back then, but my relationship with Martha had changed after, of course, I had beaten and stripped her naked in front of all the school children, and after Zena had scared her mother away. Many of the smaller kids at school who might have also been victims of Martha's bullying clung to me during recess. At the time, I had been confused as to why I had become popular.

At school, Martha stayed away from me, and I avoided her. Miss Johnson didn't let her sit by me in class. She was still mean to other kids, but when I passed her house on my trips to the market or when I took Father his lunch at the Mining Company, we gradually began to talk to each other without arguing or locking into a fight. We both remained cautious, however.

One day, I climbed a banana tree and examined many bunches until I found the very best one. The bark was very sharp, so by the time I was done, it had cut me in several places on my arms and the insides of my legs.

Before I cut the bunch free, I tied it with the rope I had looped around my shoulder. I used the knife I had strapped to my waist to cut the heavy bunch loose. Finally, I carefully lowered the yellow bananas to the ground.

I carried the heavy fruit on my shoulder back to my village, where I pulled the bunch apart. I washed them to remove all the dirt, then rubbed each one dry with clean rags Zena had given me along with the largest basket she had. Once I was done, I set off for Bomi Hills to sell my bananas.

I always sold more than the other girls who brought bananas to the market. Someone else had picked theirs for them, usually a boy who could climb a banana tree. Boys were never careful when selecting them. I was. Too green didn't appeal to those who wanted to eat them now. Too yellow, and people would only buy one or two, because the rest would brown quickly.

I picked the ones with a tinge of green on their ends and bright yellow on their sides. Because of the extra care I took in picking, washing, and drying my bananas, I was the last to arrive at the market, but this was not a problem. People who liked my bananas waited for me. They knew that mine were the best.

I was close to Martha's house when she called out, "Hi, Jabonkah!"

Because I balanced the large woven basket filled with bananas on my head, I was careful not to move too fast.

I knew Martha could not balance things, because I had seen her carry a big load of clothes in her arms. She could have made a bundle and put them on her head. I walked proudly the short distance from the road to her house. Her sister and two little brothers sat and watched me. They never seemed to help their mother with the work of the house.

They all stood.

Martha raised her arms. "Let me try."

She wanted to take my basket.

"That's easy."

I took a step backward to avoid her reach. "You would drop them and make spots on my bananas. When I come back," I pointed to her smallest brother, "you can put him in the basket and give him spots if you drop it."

The littlest boy shook his head and said, "I don't want spots," then ran inside the house.

Martha came close to me. She smelled like flowers. I used the rough, sandy soap the missionaries gave us every time they passed through our village and talked about God, the devil, and a dead man named Jesus who was invisible. She stared at my basket. I turned my head side to side to show her how well I balanced. I squatted, showing her something else I could do.

I thought she was going to grab my basket, but she surprised me and poked the long fingers of both hands into each of my dimples.

"How did you get those holes?" Martha said, then shoved her fingers harder until she jammed them against my teeth.

I recalled that Martha had been mean to me and had called Zena a stupid bush woman. I had to mumble because Martha left her fingers poked in my cheeks.

"I took two sticks from the fire and held them where your fingers are."

"No you didn't."

I tried to nod, but the balance of the basket would not allow it, so I mumbled again, "I did too."

"Well, I don't believe you."

I stepped back and turned toward the road. "You're just afraid," I said. I didn't look back, but if I had, I knew her eyes would be round with doubt. "You are too!"

"I'm not either," she said in her loud, mean voice.

After I arrived at the market, I quickly forgot about Martha. I stopped in front of the first store, where they always bought some of my bananas. Next, I walked to the big market and stood with the other children who had dirty, spotted bananas.

I set my basket down, took the best banana, and cradled it like Zena did with me when I was sad. I ran up to the people who passed and told them how perfect and clean this banana was. If they were undecided, I showed them the scratches I had gotten climbing the scaly tree. This usually worked on those who were unsure, perhaps they felt sorry for me, *this poor little bush child*. I always sold my bananas, except for the ones I ate because I was hungry.

The next day, Father came home and already had his belt out. I was helping Zena scoop rice from the black kettle. I held the bowl. "Jabonkah!" Father yelled. My hands began to shake.

Zena clasped my hands, so I would not drop his rice. She said, "What now Jabonkah?"

I suspected that Martha must have burned her face making dimples, but I didn't have time to tell Zena. Father grabbed me by my neck and squeezed so hard that I saw blackness. He ran with me and shoved me against the wall of the hut. Zena yelled, "Please, John Henry." But she and I both knew

Father would never stop what he had started.

Mama Kama came out from the hut and looked at me, then at Father. I saw the shadow of his arm on the wall as he raised it. The buckle burned my skin. I began to cry. Father stuck me over and over and over.

"Sackey, you are going to kill that girl," Mama Kama finally said. "Just give her away if you don't want her."

Father stopped. "She is worthless."

I fell to my knees.

He threw his belt at me and went inside.

Zena fell down beside me. She carefully lifted me into her arms, hugging and rocking me. Her tears fell on my face. So often it was I who had held Zena after Father had beaten her.

"Zena, where's the salt!"

"Coming, Sackey," Mama Kama said. Her voice tried to soothe him.

Zena picked me up and carried me to her room. We passed Father. He didn't look up from his dinner. She turned, closed the door with her foot, and laid me on my stomach. She fanned my wounds to cool them, then she laid a cool cloth over my back and pressed to stop the bleeding, as I had done for her so many times.

"Zena...I am worthless...he said it."

"No worthless, just Jabonkah; different and too many words."

I woke to the buzzing of large flies, the ones that bite cows and walk around on dead animals, laying their eggs. I was neither of those. I eased up off the bed. My head hurt more than my back. I had no tail to swish the bugs away, so I moved slowly, side to side, kind of like the cows that can twitch their skin to drive away the bugs.

As I stood, the cloth still clung to my back. I reached behind, tugging and pulling slowly. My head reminded me that it hurt more. I whimpered and took a deep breath, preparing to rip the sheet away in one strong pull.

I yanked and screamed then plopped face down on the bed. Darkness filled my head. Flies were biting me, and that made me realize I was still alive. I stood again, determined to find Zena. Father might have been in the other room and might have wanted to add to my misery, so I crawled out Zena's bedroom window.

She was not in front of the hut. She might be with Grandfather in his hut, but I avoided him. Zena had said he had been cursed to blindness. Naturally, I didn't want any of his curses driving into me. Being left handed was bad enough.

An empty bucket sat just outside the entrance to the hut. It had not rained for some time. This could have been Zena's way of telling me to pull water from the river or that she was there. I put the empty bucket on my head and walked stiffly, taking short gasps with each breath.

The sun burned my back as if it were on fire. The thought of sitting in the cool water, in the shallows, floating on my back with my face in the sky, came to mind. I would stay a short time if Zena was not there, she would wait for water.

I moved as if I was the eldest of our village. The monkeys called to me, and I replied, "I am hurt today…can't you see!" They only thought of themselves. I smelled the flowers, the decay of some animal, and the sunbaked ground where the trees and brush had been cleared to plant a garden, probably potatoes, cucumbers, and tomatoes. Whoever did this was foolish. There was no water for them when the plants got thirsty. Father knew better, because he told us to plant our garden within the rice field, where it remained moist longer after the rains had stopped.

Once I was near the river, I heard children laughing. I paused, listening. I didn't feel like playing, and I didn't want to be in a fight today with the kids from Bomi Hills who came to my spot in the river. But Zena needed water. I didn't have to lie in the shallows. I would get water and leave.

The first to see me were my new school friends who stayed close to me and away from Martha. "Hi Jabonkah." They yelled and waved, then came running toward me. They attracted the attention of a whole group of children, who also came running with brownish-red water splashing from under their feet. Larger boys pushed down the smaller boys and the girls as they ran past them.

A large group gathered in front of me. I could not even see the river. Martha pushed her way to the front and stood, staring at me. She had burn marks and blisters on both sides of her cheeks.

"You are going to pay for this," Martha said with a snarling voice. She stepped closer, and someone knocked the bucket off my head. Ignoring the pain in my back, I bent to grab my bucket, but the boys played with it like it was a ball, then they kicked it in the river. It started to float away.

I pushed through the bodies and tromped into the river. A foot shoved my butt, making me fall face-first in the water. The river's sharp fingers scratched my back, hurting not cooling me. I wanted to cry but wouldn't allow them to see that I was hurt and upset.

Martha grabbed my arm and lifted me. She steadied me by holding my upper arms, moving me side to side, seeming to inspect me.

"Your father did this, didn't he?" Martha said. "I was hoping he'd beat you…but not like this." She yelled at the others, "Leave her alone, or I will make you all sorry."

She ran waist deep, downstream, and retrieved the bucket that had sunk and tangled in brush.

"She's a witch; don't help her."

"Yeah, look what her father did, because she's a witch."

I could not face them. My chest heaved in and out with hatred. Martha came close and took my hand, holding my bucket that was full of water. She led me to the start of the trail, and we stopped, looking at each other. My anger for Martha flew away.

With the bucket on my head, I walked away in silence but soon saw chunks of red clay whizzing by me, crumbling into small pieces as they hit the ground. The boys could have hit me if they wanted. I stepped quickly, spilling water, hoping there would be enough left for Zena.

I saw my village and wanted to get to Zena faster, so I left the trail and took a shortcut. I guess I wasn't being careful where I was walking, because I stepped in a hole and tripped. The bucket went flying. I landed on my chest. I lay thinking about what hurt and what didn't. Only my ankle flamed with pain. My back still hurt, of course. I stood on my left foot and hopped toward our hut. The jolting up and down jarred my back and ankle and made everything hurt more. I called out for Zena.

She appeared from Grandfather's hut and ran to me. She grasped me, picked me up, and carried me near our hut, where she sat me down next to the mortar in the shade of a palm.

"My ankle is broken," I said with gasping breaths. The expression on Zena's face made me more concerned. She fingered the swollen and crooked ankle. "It hurts a lot." I cried out, now in great agony. I had forgotten about the pain in my back from the beating Father had given me until I lay down on the ground that was biting hot, even in the shade. I sat up and squealed like a frightened baby pig.

Zena tried to leave my side, but I grabbed her arm. "Where are you going?"

She twisted free of my grip. "To get Grandfather," she said.

I watched her flee from me, making my pain worse. I leaned back with my hands and arms supporting my weight while I compared the different sizes of my ankles. I cried more when I thought I might be forever crippled and never become a bush woman like Zena.

Zena appeared from Grandfather's hut and walked toward me, holding Grandfather's hand. He moved slowly because of his blindness.

Grandfather stood over me. I stopped suffering. His eyes frightened me. They were cloudy, like the river, but blue, and they swirled in eddies as they swished around aimlessly in his wrinkled face. My despair started again and continued to grow, telling me my life was over. What would I do with only one leg? If Grandfather carried me, and I told him where to walk, then together we could be a whole person. Zena would still love me, but how could I help her? I bawled knowing that life was over for me.

Grandfather sat on his heels. His balls sagged on the dirt. It must have felt hot as he said, "Shit," and lifted his body and his balls off the ground. He said, "Jabonkah, child of my daughter, be at peace." He stroked my cheeks, wiping away my tears. "You are such a pretty girl like your mother, and helpful to her." He moved his hands up and down my arms, touching me with a tenderness I had only known from Zena.

"You have such strong shoulders," he said, rubbing them. His breath was sour with the palm wine and fish that he must have just had. "You will become a great bush woman, just like your mother and grandmother and great grandmother." He kept talking, and I listened to his low voice, which seemed to vibrate inside me like the drums of Christmas.

I stopped crying. Grandfather kept talking.

"Zena tells me of all that you can do." I looked at Zena. Her arms were crossed. She seemed worried. I started to cry again.

"Hush, hush," Grandfather said. He patted my shoulders. "Zena will make you dumboy, and you can have as much as you can eat."

Zena nodded. I stopped crying. I thought about fried dumboy. I didn't notice that Grandfather had shifted his hands down my right leg and held my ankle.

I felt then heard a crack like a dry branch snapping, giving me great pain. I yelled like a drowning monkey. Grandfather had tricked me. I scooted away and tried to stand but could not, so I crawled to Zena. She picked me up and held me by my bottom, draping me over her shoulder, careful where she placed her hands on my back. My ankle was better after

Grandfather had pulled on it, but I was hurting in another way now.

"Zena, why don't the children like me...and...and... Father?" I began to cry once more but softly this time. My insides ached, and I no longer felt hungry. Pangs of grief pierced so deeply I just wanted to curl up and sleep. I looked back at Grandfather. He looked lost.

"Am I cursed like Grandfather? Will I go blind? Maybe I am cursed because of him, and that's why everyone hates me."

"Everyone, Jabonkah?"

I dropped my head on her shoulder and breathed out a sigh. "Not you."

"Grandma Crowcoco?" Zena rocked me.

I sighed again. "No, Zena, not her. But everyone else hates me."

"Was teacher mean to you?"

I could see Miss Johnson's warm smile in my mind. "No, Zena. But the kids at the river were."

"All of them?"

I remembered Martha, who had retrieved my bucket, and the little children, who came near to me at school and who had also come near me at the river.

"No, Zena." I felt my stomach growl, then thought of the dumboy. I leaned back to look in her eyes. "You don't have to make me dumboy. It takes so long, and you need to cook for Father, so he will not be angry."

"He eat dumboy too."

# 21
# Red Pepper

Somehow I seem to remember more painful events from my past than the isolated, pleasurable ones. Perhaps this is normal when life was more of a struggle to be survived, rather than a pleasure to be enjoyed. I did adore so many simple things. My love for Zena and my heartfelt connection with the natural world were the freshest and deepest joys I recall.

I tried not to repeat behaviors that brought painful consequences. For instance, I learned not to steal when my aunt, from Father's side, complained to him that I had stolen from her a single piece of Chiclets gum. This happened during the rainy season of my eleventh rice field. It was the first and last time I stole anything.

It had been raining for so long, the swift flowing water ate away the soil and left deep scars in the roads and trails. The adults stayed in their huts and visited each other, but I continued to play, as if the sky were filled with yellow sunshine instead of a continuous downpour of gray rain.

Large wet beads drummed a rhythm on my head. Soft pebbles fell from the sky, slapped on leaves, and splashed in puddles, echoing their music throughout the bush.

I was playing hide-and-seek with two girls from my village who were seven and six rice fields, respectively. My aunt was in Father's hut for dinner and most likely for the rest of the evening, so I decided to hide in her hut.

Going into huts other than your own was against the rules of hide-and-seek and forbidden in our village. But I was hungry, and in my own hut, I would not be allowed to eat until all the men, then the women, had finished. This particular evening they were taking their time, not wanting to jump streams of water in the blinding rain.

As I entered my aunt's hut, my body felt lighter, as if I had taken off the heavy coat of rain. I snooped around. Her hut was old, and she had no man to provide for her. She helped in the rice fields but moved slowly. She could barely swing a machete. Father provided for her and others in our family, but they had to work.

My aunt had no food, but she had a clear jar that was half-full of white Chiclets. She would not miss one, I thought. I unscrewed the top, took a piece, then placed the jar on the table. I put the sweet, smooth, rocklike gum in my mouth; at the same instant, my aunt walked in. She seemed surprised, and I was scared. I swallowed the Chiclets whole. I was disappointed that I hadn't gotten to crush the hard shell into crumbs. She seemed to suspect I had done something wrong, and there were only a limited number of possibilities in her barren hut.

She came to the center of the small room, near the table. I scooted to the left to hide her jar of gum. She tried to look around me. She moved slowly, and I shifted positions with her. "Jabonkah, standstill, or I will get John Henry." I stilled, so she could see her gum jar. I wanted to run, but there were few places to hide from Father.

She sat in her chair. It creaked and wobbled with her weight. I hoped it might break and fall, but the chair held. She spilled her fat breasts onto the table and reached for the gum jar. I could have scooted it closer but knew not to touch what was not mine.

Leaning back with the jar in hand, she said, "If even one is missing, I will tell John Henry." I knew the count would be one less and knew Father would beat me for taking it. Her large knuckled fingers unscrewed the lid. She dumped the white gum on the brown table, as if they were more important to her than money. "Come here. Stand closer." I moved next to her.

She used one finger with a long, curved, yellow nail and began to sort the gum in piles of five. Her hand shook as she moved them on the table, which had been smoothed by years of use and stained black by drops of grease and smears of palm oil.

After she had finished counting, she glared at me with poisoned eyes. "You thief! John Henry is right. You are worthless! And now a thief, too!"

Old or not, she reached quickly and grabbed my left ear, nearly ripping it from my head. She dragged me into the rain, stomping straight through large, deep puddles. She entered Father's hut, and she shoved me to the floor. I fell at the right side of Father where he sat at the table.

"That witch stole from me!" My aunt stood with her hands on her round hips, elbows pointing out, and glared at Father. I lay flat on my stomach with my head lifted, waiting for his reaction. "She is worthless. Why do you keep this child?"

Father stood. His chair fell backward on the floor with a sharp crack. His hands flew to his belt. He drew it from around his waist with a snapping sound that made me flinch, then he slammed it on the table.

"John Henry. Please no," Zena cried out.

His face swung to his left and his eyes seemed to throw fire on her as if they were as hot as the sun, melting Zena like a glob of white pig fat in a smoking skillet. She covered her mouth with her hands.

Father looked at me and said, "Stand up, you witch!"

He reached down, grabbed my shoulders, placing me on top of the table, then forced me to lie on my back where they had been drinking coffee. Cups scattered across the table and some fell to the floor.

"Zena, get the pepper."

Zena hesitated but not for long. I knew he would beat her if she refused to obey, and he would still do what he wanted to me.

"I'll teach you not to steal," Father said, spit flying from his mouth. She set the red pepper beside me.

"Zena," I said, with my hands in the air reaching out, but Father shoved her away, causing her to fall.

Lying on the floor, Zena said, "John Henry, please. Do this to me. She learn. I teach her."

Father stomped his foot at Zena, as if she were an animal he wanted to frighten away. "Quiet, woman, or I'll pepper both of you."

I twisted and moved my head back and forth. Father slapped my stomach then held me with his huge hand. He forced red pepper into my mouth, up my nose, and into my eyes. I choked and howled in terrific, burning pain.

"Get your hands off me. You bore this witch!" I heard the sickening sound of a fist hitting a face, Zena's to be certain.

I could not breathe. I was blinded. I puked up bile from an empty stomach, probably the Chiclets, too. Everything burned. I heard kicking, what had to be Father's hard shoe striking Zena. She groaned as air left her.

Father spread my legs and poked gritty pepper inside me. It burned with great pain and horrible humiliation. My father was setting my body in flames without even as much concern for me as a common animal, a dog.

He slipped me off the table and forced me to walk, striking the belt across my back, yelling, "You are a worthless whore. I should just kill you!" He shoved me out the door of the hut.

I fell on my back, then rolled over and over and over, not knowing where I hurt more. I rubbed mud in my eyes and filled my mouth and nose, but then Father grabbed my arms and made me stand. Father began beating me with his belt, driving me to the river, maybe to drown me. I started to run toward what I thought was the direction of the river.

I knew my way in the darkest of nights by just following the sound, especially now as the waters raged with the rains. Father was going to drown me like he had drowned the dog that had bitten his sister's leg. I cried in desperation. My insides felt inside-out. Father had no rope, I thought, or rice bag filled with stones to tie around my neck. I could swim away, unless he held me under the water, and he would. Boys in my village had told me that Father had drowned a baby who breathed but could not move.

He quit hitting me with his belt and no longer chased me, but I continued to run.

"Jabonkah!" It was Zena. I stopped and waited for her. She lifted me up and placed me down on my back. The rain drenched my face. I reached up for her. "Not now. Lie still." I did as she instructed. I opened my mouth and let the rain fall in. She forced each eye open, rinsing it. "Hold water in mouth." She clamped my jaw shut. "Sit up." I did. "Drive water through your nose." I tried to shake my head, but she held it. "Don't swallow!" She had read my mind.

I gagged, but I did it. Water shot out my nostrils. The burning sensation lessened. Zena let go of me. I held my head back and opened my mouth for the rain. Zena fed me water from cupped hands, some I drank, some I forced out my nose again. She spread my eyelids open and let the rain beat on my eyes. Next, she pulled my legs apart and packed soothing mud where father had filled me with pepper. The burning on my tender insides was intense, but not as painful as the burning in my eyes and nose.

Father's words echoed in my mind like the splattering rain on the leaves and ground; "I should just kill you," he'd said. Sadness beyond all I had ever known left me weak. Sobbing, I no longer felt the pain of pepper. My heart grieved separation from Zena in death or even if given away would kill me.

"Zena, let's run to...," I didn't know a place. "We must leave Father before he kills me or you." I could not see Zena. I reached for her head, holding it in my hands. "Please, don't let Father kill me...or drive me away."

Zena picked me up. "Man rules. You must learn."

# 22
# My Zena

A blue pickup truck rumbled and squeaked as it entered our village. A trail of dust followed it, rose above the trees, then faded into a patchy blue sky. The truck circled the area where Zena and I were boiling water for rice. There was so much dust that it seemed as if the tires were grabbing handfuls of dirt and throwing it at us. A storm-like cloud of red rained down, coating our sweaty skin with grit. I all but closed my eyes. I had to see this unusual arrival that interrupted our work of making supper and ended my thoughts about how large my leftover portion of rice might be.

The truck stopped close to where I was sitting. Looking up, it was hard to see the face of the person who sat across from the driver and whose head nearly touched the ceiling, but it had to be Father.

Sitting on my heels, picking weevils from old rice, I held my breath and waited for the dust to settle. The powdered earth that drove up my nose reminded me of digging cassava for an entire day.

If it was Father, he should be pleased that we were using the remaining rice from last year's harvest before using this year's new rice. I had just had my twelfth rice harvest, so I was twelve rice fields. We always tried to please Father, especially when Zena insisted, so I really was trying to please Zena, who worried more about Father and his anger than I did.

A truck arriving with Father in the front seat was not rare. In the past, trucks had brought large things from Bomi Hills that could not be carried by hands or on our heads: bales of rice sacks, pots, tables. But never had one come so close to me and stopped.

With a rusted squeak, the passenger-side door opened and stayed open. Without words, Father jumped out, grabbed my right arm, then dragged me to the opening of the truck. He slipped his hands under my arms and lifted me. He plopped me on the tattered seat next to the driver, who moved the metal stick that stood on the floor in between my dangling legs.

Father jumped in and banged his door closed. The driver pulled the metal stick back, which made a terrible, grinding growl under my feet. When he finished, the shiny black knob bumped my left knee. The truck jerked forward, bounced, and squeaked. I tried to squirm to look back for Zena through the missing rear window, but Father grabbed me and forced me to sit on my bottom.

Dirt made the seat slippery. I tucked my hands into the crack of the cushion behind me; otherwise, I would have fallen onto the holey, rusted floor, through which I could see the red ground running along with us.

Many times I bounced so high in the air that I was flying just like a bird. Father used his big hand to swat me down, like a bug that was annoying him. Actually, I was grateful for Father's swats. I didn't want to land on the metal stick the driver used to make grinding noises.

Heat from the motor covered my legs, bit the bottoms of my feet, and made me sweat more than usual. Water slid from my forehead to my cheeks, washing away my tears, making them one and the same. They were all for Zena, whom I feared I would never see again. We had never been apart, even when it was Zena's turn to be with Father; afterward, she would clean herself, then come back to me. But this was going to take much longer, maybe forever. A great sorrow filled me and made me look back at the cloud of dust that followed us. I had to run away, or I'd never see Zena again.

I jumped on the driver's shoulder and crawled around his neck like a skinny monkey, screeching just the same, because Father acted like a monkey hunter who had lost one of his catch, clawing and swearing for me to come back. I was almost out the window when I fell across the driver's arms with my hands holding tight to the door. Father was about to crush my foot with an angry grip that pulled me. I'm sure I hurt the driver with my fingernails, digging into anything. Now he was swearing with Father, and the truck was taking deep swerves as if the driver were palm-wine drunk.

"I want my Zena," I said in monkey crying. I knew that she must be crying, too, knowing she would never see me again. A devil possessed me. I found so much strength against Father that the driver stopped the truck and grabbed my arms. Father held both legs in one hand and slapped my back, mean and fast.

Eventually, I stopped struggling, and they let go. I curled on the seat between them, lost and dead to wanting to live. Inside my mind I could see Zena, pulling her hair out and kicking her legs on her bed. I could only sob and hurt now. I was too weak to fight anymore, but Father sat me up and threatened to hit me if I moved.

If Father had wanted to kill me, the truck would have gone deep into the bush, where he could tie me to a tree and leave me for the animals to eat. Instead, we passed Bomi Hills and traveled toward the ocean in the direction of Monrovia.

With each jarring bump and from every hole in the road, my body shook as if trying to wake me to the realization that now I would have to depend on myself and not Zena. I *was* a bush woman. I had lived twelve rice fields. In two more, I would be the wife of the ugly, old man who had bought me four rice fields ago, after I had returned from the Society. I imagined that whatever was to come had to be better than living under the rule of that man or any man.

But Zena, my Zena. I curled with my forehead touching my knees. A dark chill made me shiver. Thinking that I could not live without Zena, I sprang to my knees and began to crawl out where there was no window. Using only one hand, Father grabbed what seemed like my entire body and forced me to sit.

"Where are we going?" I cried.

Zena had tried to show me how to live in a man's world without being beaten. She had told me, repeatedly, "Too many words, Jabonkah." But I could not control my thoughts or my words. They were always in me, thick smoke in my head, burning like dry grass that could no more be stopped than I could stop thinking and talking about what I thought. Zena could not have done any more to keep me silent, to get me to accept that I lived in a world where the man ruled over his kingdom and his women.

Days ago, I had rebelled against Father for the last time. Father had beaten Zena for no reason. I had pounded on his back with my fists, but he wouldn't stop, and after he had knocked me to the floor, I crawled to his leg and bit him like a dog. He had kicked me away, also like a dog, so I had run outside, grabbed the pestle, returned, then struck him.

The pestle had been too awkward to swing. I had attempted to strike Father in the back of the head, but my enraged swing had fallen short. I had struck him in the middle of his bony spine. This had upset him even more, but I hadn't cared.

I understood his choices—kill me or give me away. To allow him to rule me meant I would have to stop loving Zena. My love for her made me want to protect her. She had tried many times to shelter me, which only resulted in more beatings for her.

Now the trees were gone from view. I tried to sit taller in the seat to peer over the front of the truck. We were entering the edge of the city. The stink of rot and decay of too many people relieving themselves too close to where they lived filled the cab.

I had been in Monrovia twice, both times to buy rice sacks. I had functioned as a rock with hands. I had sat in the back of the truck to keep the rice sacks from falling out or blowing away. Father would have been very angry if I had allowed one bag to escape.

We were not here to buy rice sacks. Harvest was over. I decided to defeat Father at whatever his plan for me might be. I would not allow him to crush my spirit beyond what he had already done. I sat up on my legs. I was a strong bush woman, capable of taking care of myself. I wiped my face clean with my hands, rubbing them on the edge of the seat where its stuffing was coming out. Although my life seemed useless without Zena, Father must have been satisfied with my pain. It probably made him happy, perhaps for the first time. I knew he would be even happier if I kept crying. I decided not to anymore, no matter what happened.

# 23
# You Can Have Her

The road was smooth now. Three tall, thick, black lines rose in the blue sky. The smell of the sea, its salty brine, filled the cab of the truck. It reminded me of when Zena and I soaked fish in salt before we dried them in the sun. I sat up on my knees. I was curious about what Father would do with me.

An enormous ship, like the one that sank with all of those people on it, hid the ocean. Never had I seen anything this large. Many people, more than I had learned to count even if they all stood still, swarmed like disturbed ants. Large poles, the size of our tallest trees, dangled massive boxes in the air that moved closer to the ground, where bare-chested men, shiny with sweat, waited with their arms raised.

There was so much to see that I forgot about the outside pain, where Father had slapped my back, but not the inside pain of losing Zena. All of this movement didn't make sense. I wanted to get out and see why everyone moved with such confusing purpose. I understood the way Father wanted us to harvest his rice field, but this was wonderfully different.

A loud squeak came from under the truck as it slowed to a stop. Father opened his door, which allowed a cool breeze to flood in. He grabbed my arm, as if it were a tree limb that he was taking to a wood pile. I stepped quickly on my toes but fell short of his long steps.

Father, with me still in his grasp, approached a group of people. I attempted to see each person, but Father bounced me so much I only got quick glimpses: black women, who held flowered umbrellas, and black men, who wiped their foreheads with small white cloths. Dressed in solid colors of white and black, these people were obviously not tribal and not like the people of Monrovia.

They held their hands above their eyes, reminding me of a soldier's salute. They seemed bothered by the sun and its heat. Several women had yellow, shimmering strings around their necks—a necklace. I remembered them from a picture in the big book Grandfather used to wipe himself. Crosses hung from their necklaces, like the missionaries who had visited our village. Yes, they were missionaries, but these people wore very nice clothes.

Father stopped in front of them. I thought he might know them and had something to say, but he just stood, saying nothing. I counted ten, seven women and three men.

They were all beautiful in their new clothes. They had kind eyes like Miss Johnson, my teacher, and skin smooth like a baby, not dry and wrinkled. Their fingernails were even clean. Several held books, a Bible. I had seen one before with its yellow letters on a black-leather cover.

Father seemed uncertain, even a little afraid. I must have given him a strange look, because he hit me in the back of the head. I fell to my knees, then looked up at the missionaries.

One of the men jumped forward and stood next to me. He wore a beard but shaved his upper lip. "Sir, this is a child of God. Jesus said, 'Let the children come to me.'" He reached and took my hand. I stood. He pulled me close to his side. His black pants were hot from the sun.

"Her? She is worthless." My father pointed at me as he spoke. "And she is a witch."

A tall, slender, beautiful woman with silver-black hair squatted in front of me. She smelled of some new flower I didn't know. I smiled at her. She seemed kind, like Zena, but when she spoke, a shudder passed down my shoulders to the bottom of my feet. Her voice was sharp and made me think of a machete that could hack through the thickest vines. "Tell me your name," she said.

I didn't like the way she narrowed her eyes, pressing them tight at the corners, just like Father did when he looked at me. I pushed my back against the man's legs. I would have stood between them, but my head came to his waist.

She reached for my hands. The smile she had been wearing was more like a mask. It changed to a frown that matched hidden lines in her face. I turned sideways in the slot of the nice man's pants. I refused to touch her pinkish-colored palms. The man, between whose legs I hid, covered my shoulder with his hand and squeezed gently. "Tell, Mother Stevens your name, child."

"Jabonkah," I murmured.

She clutched my chin and pulled my head toward hers. She squatted lower, forcing me to look at her. "Say it again."

Her eyes were big, pure white on the outside and black in the center—deep, as if there were no bottom.

"Jabonkah," I said quickly. Her hand continued to hold my chin.

"That's better. Now tell me what it means."

"Maggie, please. The child is shaking," the man said.

I pressed even harder against him.

"Oh, child, are you afraid of me?"

I wanted to say yes, but Father interrupted.

"What her name means is no matter," Father said, in his deep, annoyed voice.

"It does to me, sir," Mother Stevens said. She looked at him with eyes that Father would have beaten Zena and me for using. How could she do this, I wondered?

"I don't think it has meaning; and if it did, why would anyone care?" Father said.

"God remembers," I said proudly, feeling safe next to this strange man. I looked at Father like the missionary did but only for a moment, long enough though that I felt a power over him I had never felt, a freedom I had never known. I smiled at Mother Stevens. She let go of my face, stood, and stepped close to Father.

"She has a lovely smile, the cutest dimples, and she's strong."

"Well, do you want her? You can have her. She is useless to me." Father looked at me, cold and indifferent. He said, "I don't want her."

I tried to glare at him again, but a sickness filled my body and my face was too weak to move. I knew he hated me. But to hear him say that he did not want me to a stranger with such determination cut marks inside me that his belt buckle never had. I turned my face into the man's smooth pants. He put his hand on my back and patted it, making it difficult not to cry. I tried not to think of Zena. I wanted to run back to her, but Father would have never let me stay if I did get to my village. He might even tie a rock-filled sack around my neck and drown me in the river.

I didn't watch but heard Mother Stevens ask, "When was she born?"

Father said, "May 6, 1948."

It was the first time I'd heard my birth date. Mother Stevens pulled on me, and the man pushed me gently away.

"Jabonkah, I will call you Jeanette. Jeanette Stevens."

She drew me into her long, black skirt that was smoother and lighter than I had thought it would be.

"Her name is Jabonkah Sackey," Father said, with irritation in his voice.

Mother Stevens pushed me aside and stepped close to Father, closer than any woman should. She examined him, as if *she* were a man, and said, "Then take her back to the bush."

He backed up from her.

My mouth opened with amazement—he seemed afraid of her. Then he said, "Jeanette sounds good. Yes, that's a good name." He turned away.

He hurried toward the truck, fearing, I thought, that Mother Stevens would change her mind. I might never see him again and this was okay, but knew I would never see Zena. This hurt more than all the beatings I had ever had.

I wondered if no one had told Mother Stevens this was a man's world. She made Father act as if she were white and a man. I wanted to be like Mother Stevens, free of "the man rules." I must have smiled at her.

She said, "Child, God has delivered you from the wilderness. You *should* be smiling."

I thought she was confused. It was Father who had brought me here, not God.

# 24
# All I Had but Not Mine

Mother Stevens seemed tired. The rest of the missionaries did, too. She kept yawning. She waved her right hand in front of her face as if she were trying to ignite embers into flames.

After they had collected all of their bags, we rode in automobiles—my first time in anything other than a truck. I got squeezed between Mother Stevens and the man with the beard. Mother told me I smelled. She inspected both sides of my hands and commented on how crusty and rough they were. The insides of her hands were soft and had shades of pink and lacked the calluses and the scars of a bush woman. She must not pound her own rice or stir her own dumboy or make her own fires, I thought.

The car stopped in front of a large house, the kind that was made of wood and of a size that only people who might own more kingdoms than Father would have. When we got inside, it was so clean. It made me wonder if they let chickens eat the rice and crumbs, like those that would always be on the floor at home, especially after Grandfather ate, because he spilled more food than he got in his mouth.

We walked on blankets, which were soft on my bare feet. I carried two bags so that Mother Stevens didn't have to bring any in. This seemed to please her. I walked behind her up steps that I thought might never end. I counted fifteen plus three more.

An old black woman walked slowly ahead of Mother Stevens, grunting with each step. She opened a white door to a white room with a strange, brown bed. It was not flat but had a part that went up. A sofa, I remembered. And, next to that on a small table, sat a fat green lamp that had a round, white dress that hid the light, which seemed stupid. Why not let the light be free? The floor was bare and made of shiny, yellow strips of wood from a tree that must have been very narrow.

Further into the room, the old woman opened another door, this one to a bedroom. The most beautiful bed was inside. It had a very thin cloth draped over and around it, for mosquitoes, I thought. The bed was twice the size of anything I had ever seen, and it was covered in blankets with the biggest red roses painted on the cloth.

"Jeanette, put that bag in there." Mother Stevens looked at me and pointed to the corner of the room near the top of the bed.

I was confused.

"Jabonkah, your name is now Jeanette." She put her hands on my head, separating my hair as if she had lost something. "Now, Jeanette. Put the other bag in that room, then Mrs. Abkey will bathe you." Mother Stevens pointed to another room, a bathroom.

The old woman, Mrs. Abkey, twisted around two star-shaped silver things that squeaked. Clear water came rushing out of a silver nose. It became hot water without a fire—none at least that I saw. It was so clean I wanted to drink it.

"Remove that thing, child," Mrs. Abkey said. After I had taken off my wrap, she looked at me, focusing on where I had been cut by the Society. She shook her head, seeming to question what she saw.

"Go ahead. Get in."

I had never bathed except in the muddy river. It was the first time that I realized how dirty my feet were. They seemed brown, not black, next to the white tub.

Mrs. Abkey was old, her hair more gray than black. Her hands were strong like Zena's, and she washed me with smooth, sweet-smelling soap. She used a small, white rag that turned brown. So did my water, but it was still more drinkable than river water. Her front and the sleeves of her shirt became soaked the longer and the harder she scrubbed.

"In heaven's name, sit down, child; you're going to slip." She grabbed me and almost forced me to sit. I let her as she seemed nice like Zena.

"The water is so brown. I just wanted to see if you were rubbing me white."

"No, child," Mrs. Abkey laughed, "you still have plenty of black left." As she came from her knees, she grunted, and when she stood, she pressed against her hips with her wet hands. She reached for and took the whitest towel from a shelf, opened it, then covered me.

As she wiped me dry, I bounced up and down to look in the mirror that was above a white bowl that also had stars but a smaller nose than the flat barrel I was in.

"You tickle me, child." Mrs. Abkey said. She lifted me to look in the mirror. "See, you're still black as charcoal."

I smiled at myself then stuck out my tongue. I was satisfied that Zena would still recognize me. I wanted down, but Mrs. Abkey continued to hold me.

"Where did you get those dimples?"

"Didn't get them with hot sticks," I blurted out, afraid that she might do what Martha had done.

"You *are* the funniest little girl," said with a short laugh, "of course you didn't. Now lift your arms."

I held them in the air while she wrapped me, just like Zena and I had wrapped fish with banana leaves before we roasted them. She drew the towel tight and tucked it inside itself, like a dress. Then she pushed me into Mother Stevens's room, where I stood, enjoying the tight feeling of my skin.

"Will there be anything else?" Mrs. Abkey said.

Mother Stevens lay on her bed with her eyes closed. She had removed her shoes but was still dressed in her same clothes. The pink bottoms of her feet reminded me of large tongues.

"Did she have any lice, rashes, or scales on her?" Mother Stevens said.

I was not a fish. What did she mean by scales, I wondered.

"No, ma'am, but she has been to the Society. The scars are well healed."

Mother Stevens opened her eyes and raised her head, looking at me. She had eyes like Father's. They were narrow and seemed empty, quick to disapprove.

She rested her head back on the pillow. "Well, at least she won't end up pregnant like the rest of these *bush* girls." Her voice was sharp and cut me like a knife with two edges.

I wondered if the man missionary, who had held me between his legs, needed a little girl from the bush. He seemed kinder than Mother Stevens.

"Mrs. Abkey, please unpack my things and then find that creature something suitable for a girl to wear."

Mrs. Abkey opened Mother Stevens's bags and began to put her clothes in a large dresser that had a tall mirror. I stood wondering what I should do. I had no orders. I sensed a need to please Mother Stevens. I went to the bathroom and took the bottle of lotion, which Mrs. Abkey had used on me, rubbing the slippery green oil on my hands and elbows.

I squeezed some greenish goo in one hand and smoothed the lotion evenly between my hands, then I approached Mother Stevens. Her feet were still dangling at the end of the bed. I stood on the edges of my feet and looked down at the deep cracks and dirt-stained lines that ran the length and width of mine, nothing like her feet. I sniffed the flowery aroma. It was another new smell for me.

I placed my right hand on the top of her right foot and let it slide in a soft and gentle slip. She raised her head. She surely smelled the strong aroma of the lotion. She nodded consent and leaned back.

I cupped the ball of her heel in the lathered palm of my left hand then squeezed gently. I followed the trails of her "ahs" and "mmmms," applying more or less pressure as she led me to what pleased her. I kept my right hand on top of her foot to hold it in place, while I worked through her skin and into her tight muscles. Her foot began to relax. She seemed to give in. Her right foot became heavier, and heavier still, until I held its full weight in my hands.

I switched from the heel to her toes. Mother Stevens laughed. "Careful. That tickles." I stopped momentarily, surprised by the softness of her mood.

"Who taught you this?"

I didn't answer. This was the first time I had rubbed anyone's feet, and when I realized I had never done this for Zena, a cucumber-sized pain stuck in my throat. Zena, whom I loved, I had never shown this tenderness. I was a bad daughter. I blinked back tears. Poor Zena, what would she do without me? What would I do without her?

"Keep going." Mother Stevens threw her black eyes at me. She had lifted at the waist, arms extended to support her upper body; the softness that had been in her face was gone.

"Get more lotion," she said.

I ran to the bathroom, squeezed more goo in my hand, then returned. Mother Stevens, still on her back, wiggled her left foot.

Mrs. Abkey nodded at me, to continue to please Mother Stevens, I thought. Mrs. Abkey left the bedroom. This was a new world for me where Mother Stevens ruled. Perhaps, she had come from a different kingdom.

I continued to rub her foot. Eventually, she began to breathe heavily. I slowed my strokes and lessened the pressure, then I stopped and waited. She didn't complain. I smelled my hands then sucked one finger. I sucked all of them, licking the bitter lotion from my palms, walking to the bathroom where I grabbed the lotion bottle. I went to the smaller room on my toes, careful not to make a sound as I closed the door behind me.

I lay on the sofa, which had been made into a bed with cool white sheets. Tears for Zena, my only true mother, rolled down the sides of my face. My breathing became tight. I had lost my breath. Hope drained from me, leaving me with a hollowness that would never fill again.

For the first time, I dreaded what might happen next. With Zena, life had been complete. A thousand of Father's beatings was better than missing Zena. Father's anger and rage we endured together like the coldest night, but never possessed fear of the next new pain.

Why was Zena weak and Mama Kama strong? Father still ruled her, but he never beat her, at least I didn't see him. Zena let him give me away, and this strange woman owned me. She even stole my name, which made me wonder what else I could lose.

"Stop that howling, Jeanette!"

I stopped crying and curled up like a lost baby monkey. I stuck my flowery-flavored thumb in my mouth and sucked. I clutched the bottle of lotion with my right hand; it was all I had, and it was not mine.

# 25

# Hands of a Bush Woman

The light in the room flashed on. I startled awake, finding myself in a strange place.

"Jeanette! The lotion is all gone." She held the empty bottle that she must have found in my bed.

I sat near the end of the sofa-bed with my back pressed against the wall. Before I had fallen asleep, I sucked the oily pudding from the bottle. My stomach ached afterward, all night long, and still did.

Mother Stevens stood over me with eyes that were disapproving slits. She had fallen asleep in her daytime clothes, but now she was in her sleeping gown, so she must have wakened to change. At her side, she dangled a doubled cord, squeezing it with a knuckled grip. "I was hungry," I said.

"Hungry? Then why didn't you ask for something to eat? That was mine and will be hard to replace here. Take off your top and turn around."

I knew what was coming. Those who rule beat those who don't. I thought about running, but she would grab me, and where would I go? I slipped off the baggy T-shirt Mrs. Abkey had put on me after my bath. I twisted around and laid my chest and right cheek against the cool wall.

"Oh my, so many scars, and you're still so disobedient. Are you really worthless like your father said?"

I already knew I would never amount to anything. She didn't need to tell me. From the corner of my eye, I saw Mother Stevens position her body, measure her aim, then pause. "Your heathen father lacked the power of God to save you from your wicked ways."

She slashed my back. I cried out. The pain was sharper than the heavy blow of the buckle.

"He lacked God's grace, but I shall succeed," she paused for a breath, "and he is ungodly, so how could he correct you?"

She struck me many times and spoke continually. I didn't understand most of her words, but I heard them: something about sparing the rod and spoiling the child. Father didn't talk as he beat me, except for cursing me. He did accuse Zena of being with other men while he had beaten her.

Mother Stevens stopped. I collapsed onto my bed. My back was on fire. A panther could have scratched me to cause this much pain. For as long as I was alert, she stood over me in silence.

I woke in darkness and had to pee. During my bath, I drank and drank and drank so much white water that now it hurt to hold it in my body. I didn't want to pee in the bowl that choked when it swallowed, so I crept out of the room, tiptoed down the stairs, and slipped outside. The cooler night air soothed the fire Mother Stevens had started. When I was done peeing, I stepped onto the cool concrete that ran like a ribbon along the road and houses.

I sat down and rolled, slowly, on my back, absorbing the coolness of the hard surface, grateful that it drove away some of my pain. There had to be stars above the streetlight that shone above me, but I saw none. I was learning that I didn't miss things until I no longer had them. I no longer had Zena. I missed her more than my capacity to feel. I missed the stars and my scratchy bed of dried fronds. I wondered how such great emptiness could live and grow in my small body. It had to escape. I needed it to leave me, to drive from my ears, eyes, mouth, and nose to get it all out, or I felt like I might not survive. I was tormented beyond hope.

I curled on the sidewalk. A predawn breeze carried ocean aromas, hinting of fish and salt and reminding me how Zena and I had dried our fish in the sun, using salt I bought from the store. *Would every smell remind me of Zena?* The breeze also held the hungry voices of gulls. My stomach growled. I pushed down on my middle to relieve the pain. If Zena heard my stomach talk, she knew it was time for me to eat. Often, she fed me before I even asked.

Then a warm calmness began to spread over me. It removed the sadness that Father had put in my body when he gave me away. I sat up, turning side to side, searching for the stream of warm water that flowed over me. Seeing none, I looked down at my chest. This peace was inside, comforting me.

I stood and looked in the sky for the moon. There it was round and full, hidden by the head of the streetlight. I breathed in deeply as I faced it, closing my eyes. Zena! She was praying for me! I felt her presence. She drove away my sadness and worries and reminded me of all the things that I loved, like she had reminded me of those who were nice to me.

There were so many things that I loved: My monkey friends. The smell of rice and flowers. Dumboy! Playing with Zena. I wanted to be in the rice field with her now, to smell the rice and to eat the cucumbers that grew there. I wanted to see Zena to tell her about this feeling inside me and ask her if this was what she felt when she prayed to the moon.

"Child, come in here." It was Mrs. Abkey. She stood just outside the door of the Missionary House. She was wearing some sort of dress that had long arms and long straps that tied in the front.

I didn't want to leave the spot where I felt safe and protected by some strange feeling.

"Come on, now," she said and waved. "Where are your clothes?" She planted her hands on her hips. "Hurry now, the morning is not waiting for you."

I walked slowly to her, not sure what to expect. Now close, she grabbed my shoulders and turned me. "Child...I heard that *woman* whipping you." She twisted me to the light that shone from the entry, then, with gentle finger tips, she touched the burning areas on my back. "Well, at least your skin didn't split open." She made disapproving sounds with her tongue. "What did you do, child?"

It took me a moment to recall why I had gotten this beating, beatings often came without reason. My lower stomach growled. I remembered.

"I ate her lotion." I paused then said, "You heard me crying?"

"I did, child. And so did God. We stood outside your door."

"He did? Is he still there?" I tugged at her hands. "Let's go see." She began to laugh.

"No, my bush child, he is gone."

I let my hands fall slack. "But I wanted to see him. Please, tell him to stay next time."

She laughed at me again. "Yes, I will. You can be sure of that."

She gathered me into her big arms and breasts and held me. "Forgive me, Lord, for not feeding this child." She rocked me back and forth like Zena had when I needed comforting, except this time I also felt a peace in my body that was strange and welcome. But these feelings did not come from Mrs. Abkey.

"Come, you can be useful in the kitchen. Did your mother teach you to cook?"

"Yes, yes, I can cook."

"That's what I thought. I noticed you have the hands of a bush woman."

She showed me her hands. I touched them. She had scars like mine, but hers were smooth and wrinkled, with the looseness of an old woman.

"No more hot pots and fires here in the city."

"I am a good cook," I said, staring up into her gentle brown eyes.

"I am sure you are."

# 26
# Born Again

For the months I lived with Mother Stevens at the Missionary House, she took me wherever she went. I thought that if she'd had a trained monkey to carry things and rub her feet, which I did every night, she would have been happier.

One evening, as I was standing at her side rubbing her temples, Mother Stevens said, "How did you learn this?" Her breath was minty. I liked to eat her toothpaste, too.

"It just happens, ma'am." I had learned to please her, just following her moans with my fingers, as I had the first time that I had rubbed her feet.

"Jeanette, do you know Jesus Christ?"

Of course I had heard his name. Mrs. Abkey said he follows us around, but I never saw him or heard his footsteps. "Yes, ma'am."

"Would you like him to live in your heart?"

I stopped rubbing her right temple. She turned to face me. Her eyes seemed like the deep holes in the ground where the rain rushes in but never comes out again. I looked at her. "Yes, ma'am, if you would like him to live in me." I didn't want Jesus inside my small body. He might want too much room, but Mother Stevens's whippings came from the smallest mistakes.

She sat up and rose from the bed, pulling me by the arm. She forced me to kneel and placed her hands on top of my head.

"Lord, forgive this child," she said, "for her transgressions that are contrary to your will. She now kneels before you."

She lifted my chin so that I was looking into the depths where nothing returns.

"Jeanette, you must accept him freely...of your own will." She paused.

I looked at her chin.

"He is ready to forgive you of your sins."

I had heard of sins but didn't know if I had any. I figured that wanting Father to die for the beatings he had given Zena and me was a sin, but I didn't want to be forgiven for that, because I still wished it. Maybe telling Martha to burn dimples into her cheeks was a sin, and if it was, I was willing to drive that one off. Yes, and the monkey bridge that I had cut into the river. I still felt sorry for making Zena walk so far to the next crossing. I would let Jesus forgive me of these sins.

"I am ready, ma'am."

She closed her eyes, put her hands on top of my head, then forced it down. The tops of her bare feet were still shiny from the lotion I had rubbed in.

"Dear, Heavenly Father, Jeanette kneels before you. She is ready to ask for your forgiveness and ready to accept you as her savior. I pray, Father, that you show your abundant mercy and that you forgive her for her hedonistic upbringing...and obvious rebellion.

"Yes, Lord, I am trying to guide her, but I need your wisdom, power, and mercy to save her from the way of Satan and these African superstitions."

When she stopped talking to men who were not in the room—the Lord, Heavenly Father, and a man she called the savior—she began to sing, words about saving grace and one about crossing some river.

As she continued to sing, I waited for something to happen, looking at the floor for the feet of Jesus, who was supposed to come and live in my heart. I saw no feet and felt nothing.

"Listen to me!" She tapped her knuckles on my head. "Oh, dear Father, yes, I have doubts if this child is ready, but I leave her to your loving grace."

Mother Stevens pushed down harder on my head. Maybe she thought I would be more attentive if my neck were broken.

"Repeat after me, Jeanette." Mother Stevens paused. "Dear Lord Jesus." She grabbed my hair, then shook my head back and forth, like I had water in my ears. "Repeat what I just said."

I shouted, "Dear Lord Jesus," perhaps too fast and too loud, I guessed, because Mother Stevens breathed in loudly through her nose, then let out a full breath.

"Jeanette, repeat after me." Mother Stevens said, "Jesus I come freely to you, and I know that I am a sinner."

I repeated.

Mother Stevens said, "I truly believe that you died on the cross for my sins."

I repeated these and many other words very fast, because my head became so full of words that I had to spit them out just as soon as they entered.

Mother Stevens said, "In Jesus Christ's name, I pray. Amen."

I repeated.

She waited.

I waited too. It started as a chill. Something flowed into me like the river of feelings that I had experienced before. The last time was outside the Missionary House after Mother Stevens had first beaten me. Maybe it was the same spirit as before, or maybe it was this spirit of Jesus; whichever, I sensed my fears and sadness leaving me, which left me with feelings of peace. It was one of the first times I'd felt safe and had hope without Zena. I leaned forward, removing Mother Stevens's touch. I placed my hands on the floor. I was near to tears, thinking that I *could* go on without Zena, not wanting to but knowing I could.

"What have you done to me, ma'am?"

"Nothing, it is the power of Jesus Christ and his spirit that lives within you."

I was confused. Maybe this was a new spirit. "Is his spirit like a curse? Will it make me blind like Grandfather?" My legs felt weak. She lifted me to my unsteady feet. "I don't want him in me...I change my mind."

"No, Jeanette, you have been born again in Jesus Christ. Your life belongs to him."

"Well, I thought Jesus was a man, so if I've been born in Jesus, then is he a woman?" I was more confused and needed this Jesus out of me but feared it was too late.

Mother Stevens's eyes squeezed together as they did when she wanted to whip me. She pinched the top of my shoulder, hard. "Go to bed."

I left her, wishing she would answer questions as Mrs. Abkey did. I went to bed, deciding I would speak with Mrs. Abkey in the morning.

I woke to the smells of baking bread. A wet spot on my pillow caused me to wonder if I had begun to drool before or after I had smelled the bread. I crept down the stairs, quieter each time. I had learned which steps released the squawks that had been trapped inside. Disturbing Mother Stevens from her sleep was never good.

In the early morning, Mrs. Abkey always had something ready for me to eat: greens fried in palm oil; leftover cow, chicken, or pig that she sprinkled with salt; or she might have made me a small loaf of bread or a little pan of cornbread that I could smother with butter and jam. Tea. There was always tea with as many teaspoons of sugar as Mrs. Abkey would allow, usually three, occasionally four.

During the mornings with her, I found answers to most of my questions and discovered more to ask, about Jesus, the afterlife, and how Jesus healed the lame and sick. It was after these predawn lessons that I looked forward to Mother Stevens's trips.

Mother Stevens ventured far away from Monrovia and deep into the bush, mostly on Sundays, visiting the villages of those who were sick or visiting the various villages of the Bassa tribes. Mother Stevens negotiated with them to give her land for her school for boys.

We also visited Mother Holmes at her mission. Mother Stevens left me with Mother Holmes for weeks at a time, and this was fine with me. Mother Holmes was kind and never beat me. Plus, she made me peanut butter sandwiches with jelly made from strawberries and blueberries. Berries I had never eaten before. And she told me stories, amazing stories about this man called Jesus. It was hard to believe that he could walk on water, but he seemed like a very nice man to heal the blind man and save that woman from being stoned. Father would have beaten her as he did Zena.

On one trip, I hoped we were going to see Mother Holmes. But from the front seat of the car, Mother Stevens instructed me not to touch anything, especially the bodies of the lepers. I had been around those with tuberculosis, and I had tended to Zena during the many, many, many days she had the pox. She had stayed alone in the hut in our village, where the sick lived while they were recovering. I had touched Zena many times and never got her sores.

The lepers reminded me of the stories about Jesus. He had healed ten lepers, and only one of them had returned to give praise to God and to thank Jesus, a Samaritan.

I wondered if Jesus would follow us to heal these lepers. I looked out the back of the car. When we stopped, all I could see was the red dust that had been following us. It filled the car, annoying Mother Stevens because it coated her dress. Then I thought that Jesus might already be with the lepers, so I became anxious to get there in case this was the day Jesus chose to heal them.

# 27
# Over the Ocean

We parked far from the village. The driver refused to go any closer.

"Young man, this is ridiculous," Mother Stevens said to the driver. She was soaked in sweat. Dark circles under her arms had grown bigger the longer we had driven. The fine hairs around her temples were pasted to her skin.

She smelled horrible—too much perfume. Mother Stevens used just a small amount in the city, except when she visited the man at the bank. The driver had complained soon after she got into the car. He had jumped out of the car to look for the skunk he said he must have run over.

"No one goes there…and there's no road," the driver said.

Mother Stevens fanned herself with her thin Bible, which she almost always carried; in the other hand she held a beautiful rag with lace around its edges. She used it to wipe sweat from her brow and neck. She called the rag a hanky. She had never complained about the heat and sweat of the dry season, but I thought she wanted to.

She glanced out the window, turning her head, searching for a road, I guessed, that would lead to the village. "The trail *is* large enough to drive on," she said to the driver in a voice that made me worry she had brought the electric cord with her and might use it to beat him.

The driver removed the keys and hurried out of the car. He walked in the opposite direction of the leper colony to the shade.

"Well, we shall walk as Jesus did—into the wilderness." She opened her door. "Come, Jeanette."

I got out and went quickly to her side. It was a short distance for me, but she was not used to long walks.

Sad cassava fields surrounded the colony, wilted tomato plants and scroungy patches of cucumbers. Thistle grew tall everywhere. The pink blossoms were dead now, but they were full of seeds that the wind would drive and spread, choking even more of the vegetables. Father never allowed this. Zena and I pulled these plants when they were small. I never knew how terrible our fields could have become if the thistles had not been removed.

Fat locusts took flight. We disturbed those that covered the narrow path and those thick in the weeds. Mother Stevens was a city woman and seemed afraid that their spiny legs would snag in her hair. She removed a pink scarf from the pocket of her black dress and wrapped it over her head, tying it below her chin. She used her Bible to hide her face.

Locusts crept up Mother Stevens's white leg stockings.

"Get them off me!"

She fussed and walked in a funny way that made it more difficult to pick them off. Zena and I had eaten locusts many times, but we preferred them roasted. Once I had the last one, Mother Stevens reached between her legs, pulled the back of her skirt forward and gathered it tight so the locusts could not crawl under her dress.

She and I stopped once we got to the clearing that was close to the village. There was nothing for the locusts to eat where we stood. The ground was hard clay, so the locusts were no longer a problem for Mother Stevens.

From her pocket, she removed two blue squares of cloth; they had white strings sewn into their four corners. "Now, Jeanette, stay close to me." We had worn these masks when we had visited villages of those who cough horribly and who had blood stains on the fronts of their clothes.

Bony, scab-covered dogs greeted us, heads down and tails between their legs. I started to pat one on the head, but Mother Stevens jerked my arm away.

"I told you. Don't touch anything!"

I ducked, sensing her disapproval might come with a blow. Father's had.

"Come here." She put the mask over my face. "Hold still." The mask was too big, and it covered my ears and almost hid my eyes.

Small and large children soon appeared with their hands out. Their ribs showed, and I could have counted each one, if I had wanted.

Mother Stevens reached into her pocket and pulled out slips of paper with Bible verses on them. She read the verses aloud as she gave them to the children. She took care not to touch the kids. She told the children that God so loved the world that he sent his only son to save them and give them everlasting life. I wondered if they wanted to live forever as lepers.

She and I walked closer to the huts. The children followed, eating the strips of paper that had the Bible verses. Mother Stevens opened her Bible, and it lay in both her hands. She continued to read from the Bible, stopping at each hut, reading the same verse over and over. "For God so loved the world that he gave his only begotten son, that whoever believes in him should not perish but have everlasting life."

Those in the hut, whom I could see, turned their faces toward us as they sat or lay on the ground. No one came out. Some huts were very dark inside, so I didn't know if anyone heard Mother Stevens. I followed behind her, sad for the disfigurement of faces, toes, and feet. At one hut, the sun shone on a woman whose eyes reminded me of Grandfather's cloudy blue eyes. Most of her nose had fallen off. Her dark nostrils stared at me. They were another set of eyes. She sat with her legs crossed. On one foot, her toes were missing. She wore rags that fitted her loosely for clothes.

Mother Stevens walked ahead. I stopped. A deep sadness wanted to fight me, take me to the ground, and rip my clothes off. I could never endure life like this. I was thankful I had my nose and toes. I was thankful to be Mother Stevens's daughter, even with my sadness of being without Zena.

I remembered the story Mrs. Abkey had told me about Jesus, how he had not been afraid to touch the lepers and how he had loved them and healed them. Something made me step closer, even though the smells that came from the hut reminded me of a rotting animal. Flies buzzed in the air and crawled on the old woman's face and the rest of her twisted body.

She had once been beautiful, with high cheekbones and large eyes that were the shape of a smile. They still smiled in blindness.

"Whose shadow hides my sun?" the old woman said, exposing her red gums and few remaining teeth. She turned her head back and forth, trying to connect with my face. She stopped searching. She found me and stared with a peaceful face, gentle as a morning sky.

"Do you love me?" she said.

I hesitated, then said, "Jesus loves you."

"But do *you* love me?" She waited for an answer.

I saw both the woman she had been and the woman she was now. I said, "Yes, I love you."

She dipped her head with a nod and said, "Then come...hold me."

Mother Stevens was out of sight.

I remembered her harsh words about not touching the dogs or these people. Yet some force pulled me from the front and pushed me from behind, making me step closer to her. As I did, I glanced down the row of huts. Mother Stevens was not in sight.

"Jesus is the bread of life," I said, remembering the words Mother Stevens used as I moved still closer.

The old woman raised her hands toward me and said, "Come in then and give me the bread of life."

I looked for Mother Stevens once more. I remembered Jesus said that he who gives to those in need gives to him, or something like that. I wanted to give to Jesus. He cared for the lepers. I entered the old woman's hut.

"Welcome to my home." She turned her body, and her overcast-colored eyes followed me. "You're not afraid?"

I sat next to her. She smelled of poo and pee. "Yes, I am, but God is with me." The sun shone on the side of her head, revealing sores and scabs, splotched among patches of gray hair. I reached slowly and rested my palm and fingers on top of her wilted hand.

"You're left handed. Are you cursed with an affliction I cannot see?" She rotated her hand, entwining her remaining fingers with mine. "What is your name, child?"

"Jabonkah," I said in a whisper.

"Ah, yes. *God is with you.*" She paused while she placed her other hand on mine. It had no fingers and was wrapped in a stained bandage. She rubbed the rough cloth over my hand. "You're not cursed." She blinked, but only her right eye moved. She smiled and said, "Ah, and one day, Jabonkah, you will go over the ocean." Then she closed her right eye and began to hum. It was not the song Zena hummed, but I wished it was.

Tears tumbled down my face. Joy flooded my heart, similar to the joy I had felt when being with Zena. I placed my arm around her bony body. I thought about crawling into her lap, but she seemed as fragile as a butterfly's wing.

"Jeanette! Come out of there!"

The old woman resisted my efforts to free my hand from hers. "Who is this?"

"Mother Stevens," I said.

"She is not your mother. Why call her so?"

"Jeanette, come out of there—now!"

"Go, child. She tries to rule you." She released me and hunched forward and rocked back and forth. "Jabonkah," the old woman said as I stood, "love is my freedom." She stopped rocking and took one last look, searching for my presence, then finding me said, "Faith is your freedom."

Mother Stevens made me sit alone in the backseat of the car. I was sure she was waiting until we returned to the Missionary House to beat me. But first she told Mrs. Abkey to soak and scrub me in a bathtub that the employees of the Mission House used. Mother Stevens had my clothes burned.

Mother Stevens might have beaten me, but she didn't. She told me I was a bad girl for not listening to her, and she made me sleep on the floor in Mrs. Abkey's room. She didn't want to be in the same room with someone who had touched a leper. My confusion multiplied, thinking about what Jesus seemed to have wanted me to do.

Perhaps the old woman meant that I would be going to Heaven when she said I would go over the ocean. Maybe I was going to die soon. This brought happy images of roads made of gold, a place where there is no more pain, where Jesus lives with the lepers.

# 28
# The Lost Boy

Mother Stevens used Mother Holmes's boarding school as a model for her school, except Mother Stevens's was for boys only. She had to convince the leaders of the Bassa tribe to sell her the land she needed. She thought they should give it to her, because she was doing God's work. They had been resisting Mother Stevens, so she called them heathens, and she even said that the devil had hardened their hearts. But I wasn't sure they knew about her devil or would have cared had they known about him. Her devil wasn't nearly as frightening as the Society Devil.

I didn't understand how Mother Holmes overlooked my mistakes and fits of absentmindedness, which would have resulted in beatings if Mother Stevens had known about them. They both sang the same songs by heart, recited the same Bible verses, and they both smiled when they stood in front of the children and spoke about Jesus and his love.

"I don't want to leave Mother Holmes," I said to Mother Stevens. "I want to stay here."

We had been at Mother Holmes's school for three days, and I had attended classes with nice girls who didn't make fun of me. After school, they helped me learn to read and made certain I knew my ABCs, even if they asked me to start in the middle. I had lots of trouble reciting the alphabet backward, but they could as easily as starting at the beginning. They also gave me a pad of paper, a yellow pencil, and a book to keep—about Dick and Jane, two white children who didn't know how to *fetch* water. Yes, I fell once with a bucket of water, but I had stepped in a snake hole.

At our evening devotions, I had sat next to Mother Holmes. She put her arm around me while we sang and shared a song book, which she didn't need. She liked me like Mrs. Abkey cared for me.

As she sat on the toilet, Mother Stevens looked at me and said, "Jeanette, give me privacy."

The door and I were out of reach; otherwise she might have smacked me or closed the door. I turned my back to her. "I must stay. I am learning to cook and clean with bleach, and that will be useful once you have your school. I could help our cooks—"

"Jeanette!"

I ran from Mother Stevens's room into the amber sunlight that spread across the morning sky. I skipped and hopped to where the cooks stirred the big black pots that hung above the glowing fires. The smell of boiling oats and smoke made my stomach growl.

"Jabonkah." The woman cook, Cheayee, called to me. She refused to use my English name. "Come and set the tables."

Without answering, I skipped to the drying racks and collected an armful of plastic bowls. I hugged all the bowls I could carry, then started at the end of the table, placing them on the white-washed top. The brown benches were scooted under the tables, allowing my short arms to get close. A roof kept the midday sun off the children as they ate, but not the morning and evening suns.

Sleepy children formed lines to the outhouses. Some girls played pattycake as they sang rhythm songs. One boy, about my age, took bowls from the drying rack and began to set the middle row of tables. He didn't look at me. He was slow and not careful. His bowls were not evenly spaced.

"Hey, you." I yelled. My voice echoed in the ceiling of the roof. I pointed to the space I made between the bowls, then said, "Not so close." I pointed to his bowls that were side by side. He held his head down and acted as if he could not hear me. Then I remembered he was the boy who had been in trouble with Mother Holmes for fighting.

After breakfast, I helped with the dishes. My hands had never been so clean. When we were finished, my calluses moved around as if they would come off if I gave them a hard tug. I peeled away a loose layer of skin from the side of my hand. For a moment, I wondered if this might be the beginning of leprosy. I inspected my fingers, wiggled them. I didn't think Jesus would let me get leprosy, but I was not certain.

While the children went to their classes, I escaped to my favorite place—the swing. Knotted ropes hung from a crooked branch, and each dangling end was attached to a splintery board on which I sat. Mother Holmes had given me a Bible. The problem was—I could not read. I could have attended class with the others, but they were beyond their ABCs.

I sang songs: "Jesus Loves Me" and the "ABC" song. I swung slowly while I gazed down the red road, which brought visitors on foot and supplies by trucks. Parents also came, lonely for their children. I kept watch for a tall man and a short woman. Father was the tallest of any man, and Zena the shortest of any woman. It was impossible they would come to see me. "How would they know I was here?" I said to myself. But I continued to weave a vine of hope they might appear. The parents of the other children did. Why not mine?

I opened my Bible to read. I only knew a few words. There were lots of "thes" and "ands" which didn't lend meaning, yet these were also God's words, and they gave me comfort. I felt his presence, real as the sunshine that warmed the top of my head.

I wanted to tell everyone I met about Jesus, but all the people here already knew about him. I wanted to follow him like the disciples and devote my life to him like Mother Holmes and like Mother Stevens. Only, I had decided I would not beat children, like Mother Stevens did. Jesus never beat anyone as far as I had heard, and no one had told me a story where he had. If anyone had told me that Jesus beat children, I would have wanted to read it myself, and, since I could not read, it might be a while before I could find out for sure.

Dark figures approached. They were too far away to determine their height. I set my Bible next to me and stood. Still I could not tell if they were tall and short. Why I longed to see my Father I didn't understand; maybe because Zena could not come without him. I sat back down on the board.

Someone pushed my back. I gripped harder to keep from falling. My

Bible fell to the ground. "Hey!" I complained at first, then felt the cooling effects of the motion. I stopped with the swing when it reached the end of its arch. I turned to see who had pushed me. It was the boy who had not spaced the bowls properly on the tables.

As I fell back close to him, he grabbed the ropes near the sides of the board and jerked me to a stop. I waited. He seemed to wait, too. This made me uncertain as to what he was going to do. Maybe he wanted me off so he could swing. Still holding the ropes, he backed up. My body leaned forward at a sharp angle. I gripped tighter. I tilted so far over that my bottom wanted to slip off the board. All I saw was the dirt, and it seemed so far down. Then suddenly, he lurched into a vicious run. I held on with a deep and growing fear, one that I had never experienced on the monkey bridge. The ground became a blur. My stomach felt dizzy.

I screamed as I nearly touched the sky. Stopping, floating, I saw much farther down the road. I whooshed backward and screamed again.

The boy was in front of me. His smile lifted the corners of his mouth. He seemed happy and angry at the same time. He held his mixed grin. I swung back and forth, slowing. I no longer watched the ground or sky or even the road. Our eyes attached us. Neither of us broke away.

He grabbed my legs and stopped me with a jerk. My head bobbed front and back. I wiggled my legs. I wanted him to let go, but he ran backward, pulling me, then he let go. As I flew away from him, he turned and ran toward the border of Mother Holmes's mission and soon was on the road. He never stopped. He never looked back.

Later that same day, I asked Mother Holmes about him. She immediately counted the boys, and, after she had finished, she seemed satisfied that all of her boys were still here. She explained that in the past, lost boys would pass through, stay a few days, then leave before they were discovered. She guessed he had been such a boy.

Now, whenever I went to the swing, I watched for a tall man and a short woman—and the lost boy.

# 29
# Mother Holmes

Mother Stevens built her mission for boys, and she adopted another child— Randy. He was very tall, very black, and he made it very clear that I knew he was four years older than me. He was sixteen. I was not certain that Randy was the reason I stayed at Mother Holmes's mission until Mother Stevens's was built, but I believed it was. This was fine. Mother Holmes was kind and never beat me.

Randy smiled all of the time, seemingly happy, but I knew that he smiled because he had just gotten away with a mischievous deed.

"Mother sent you this," Randy said.

He handed me a brown paper sack with oil stains on the sides and bottom. His smile threatened to charm me. His intelligent eyes distracted me, until I noticed the glossy smear of fat on the right side of his mouth. In the past, on Sunday evenings, Mother Stevens had sent me fried chicken, usually both legs and thighs and the neck.

I opened the sack and shook it around to see the dark-brown, crusty pieces. The aroma sparked a flood of saliva, causing me to swallow.

"There is only one leg."

He shrugged and said, "I was starving. Be glad you got anything." His smile vanished and his eyes narrowed. He took a swipe at the bag, but I was quicker and too hungry for the salty, deep-fried chicken to allow him to steal the last of it.

"You're mean," I said, then ran to the storeroom where the dry foods were kept and where it was cooler. The brush had grown over the hut, covering it with shade. It was dark inside but not black. I sat on a large bag of rice and began to eat, taking my time to rip, chew, and swallow the cold meat. I savored each small bite.

Mother Holmes assigned several of the older girls to take turns helping me learn to read. I was very motivated, because we used the Bible as our reading textbook. We read mostly from the New Testament. I wanted to learn everything about Jesus.

I stayed busy during my time at Mother Holmes's mission. I helped with the chores. I woke early each day and worked beside the women. I cooked, gardened, fished, fetched water and wood, and did anything else the children needed. Work distracted me from my continual memories of Zena and Grandma Crowcoco—life when I had loved it the most.

I enjoyed being in the presence of Mother Holmes. I followed her around like an evening's shadow. Leading devotions, I listened to her recite the Psalms. She spoke them as if they were her own memories. I could not determine if she had a favorite. She rarely seemed to repeat them, but this one stuck in my mind for some reason: "Preserve me, God, for in you I take refuge."

Mother Holmes went from our morning devotions to the children's breakfast table to greet them, to staff meetings, and to oversee the delivery of supplies when the big trucks arrived. She often took time to sit with me.

One day in the storage hut, while I was praying, I looked up at the dusty beams. The morning sunlight shone through the cracks in the mud wall. Mother Holmes entered and stood in silence until I came to a break in my expressions of love for Jesus.

"You love the Lord, don't you?" Mother Holmes said. She sat next to me on a rice sack. She held a clipboard in her hand.

"Yes, ma'am, but not as good as you."

She chuckled with a deep, gentle voice. "Oh, my dear, Jesus loves us all equally.

Her eyes revealed a love for me as Zena's had. "Why does Mother Stevens hate me?"

Mother Holmes reached over and drew me into her arms. "She doesn't hate you."

"Why does she beat me? Jesus said, 'Allow the little children and don't prevent them from coming to me.'" I looked up at her. Her eyes were closed. "Jesus loved children, so why doesn't she?" She didn't answer.

"Mother Holmes?" I said. She opened her eyes. "I want to stay here with you. Why don't you adopt me? I would work hard and obey everything you said, and I'd be the best daughter ever!"

She seemed to search my face for something before she answered. "I am too old to have a daughter. Mother Stevens is much younger and will need your help at her mission."

I drew closer to her slender body. "Then, please pray for me, that Jesus finds me a new mother who will not beat me."

Mother Holmes began to rock me, and I clung to her chest like a baby monkey to its mother. She stroked my head then laid her cheek on my cornrows. "Child, place your faith in Jesus; only he can help us—according to his will."

I broke away from her, far enough to say, "But Mother Stevens says Jesus talks to her about me. And he never talks to me about me." I laid my head back down.

"He speaks to all of us through the scriptures and our prayer."

I released my grip on Mother Holmes. She let go of me. I scrambled to my knees, placed my hands, palm to palm, drew them to my lips, then closed my eyes. "Heavenly Father, thank you for Mother Holmes and her kindness for me, and if I can't be her daughter, then please drive me away to a mother who will love me like my real mother, Zena." Mother Holmes joined me on the floor. I could smell the lotion she used to make the pain in her hands go away. I looked sideways at her and smiled. She winked. A warmth and glow filled me as the hairs on my arms stood on end.

She prayed, "Heavenly Father, we are two who have gathered in your son Jesus' name. You know our needs like you provide for the birds in the fields."

I stopped listening for a moment and considered the birds I had driven away from Father's rice fields. I wanted to ask Mother Holmes if I had sinned in driving the birds, but then she began to pray about Zena. "Please be with Jeanette's mother, Zena; though she knows you not by your holy name, she shares your spirit of love with her daughter, Jeanette."

Again my mind ran to another place where Zena and Grandma Crowcoco were on their knees praying to the moon. I wondered if God was upset they did this. I whispered, "Please forgive them."

Mother Holmes finished with, "It is in your son's name I pray."

I had missed the end of her prayer. I lifted my eyes to the beams and prayed, "Forgive me, Jesus, for my sins and those of Zena and Grandma Crowcoco. They didn't know you, but they were kind to others and helped them." I forgot the rest of my prayer in my distress for the souls of Zena and Grandma Crowcoco. They didn't know Jesus, so they could not go to Heaven. But, deep inside, I felt that if they showed up at Heaven that God would not push them out; after all, God made the moon, and Zena and Grandma Crowcoco spent a lot of time praying to it.

# 30
# Fire That Melts the Stars

Eventually, the Bassa tribe signed an agreement with Mother Stevens for the land she needed to build her school for boys. The location was five miles away from Monrovia and was covered with brush and spotted with trees, which Mother Stevens paid the Bassa tribe to remove. She also paid them to dig the holes in the hard ground over which would be placed the huts you enter to poo. I guess it made sense to have a poo hut when Mother Stevens expected to have so many boys. It would make walking in the dark less surprising.

I used to believe Liberia was a man's world. Zena had always told me this, and Father always acted as if it were, but now I wondered if Mother Stevens owned the entire earth. She seemed to rule over everything, or at least she tried to.

She complained bitterly to a Bassa tribesman whom she thought was in charge. Mother Stevens was upset about how slowly the men worked. They had already been working for a week, and that was too long. Plus, she went on; they were costing her more money with each lazy day they took to complete the clearing.

She also scolded this same man for forcing the women and children of the tribe to work during the hottest part of the day. The looks she showed him reminded me of the twisted faces Father used to give Zena and me when he was upset. This older tribesman, who was missing half of his right leg, was the only man who didn't walk away from her.

He had tried to crawl to leave, but Mother Stevens was too fast for him. Once he knew that it was useless to crawl, he just looked up at her and yelled back at her in Bassa.

I sat next to the old, one-legged man and watched Mother Stevens continue to complain. I had never seen a woman this angry at a man. I'm certain that if he'd had two legs, he would have beaten her long ago.

It all stopped when two younger Bassa men came, cursed Mother Stevens, as the one-legged man also did, then carried him to the other side of the clearing, where they sat him under a tree. I could still hear him making curses, but Mother Stevens went back to the shade where she had a chair and a paper fan that she waved to cool herself.

For the final two days, the Bassa men sorted out the trees that could be used to build huts and dragged them to an area where the women and children removed the limbs and peeled the bark. After this, the men dragged the logs to the locations where they would build huts for storage, dining, cooking, and outhouses. Mother Stevens hired carpenters from Monrovia to build the many-room school hut, which was also part of the boys' dormitory, and her three-bedroom house.

Finally, the land was clear, and a celebration was to occur this night. Mother Stevens would not allow me to work in what she called "the dead heat of the day" to help the men and boys pile wood. I helped the Bassa women prepare tonight's feast, during which the huge pile of dried brush and tree limbs would be burned.

While I was cooking, I watched the lucky boys who got to help the men pile more and more and more branches and limbs in the center of the clearing. It seemed to me that the men were the happiest, because this was going to be a very big fire, and it would allow them more time to dance and to drink and to get drunk.

I knew the boys thought they were special to drink with the men, but I had tasted palm wine before, so I knew they were not. They were just stupid and pretended to like it. I guess they acted that way so that they could eat and dance before it was my turn. Boys were also like this in my tribe, and all over the world, I guessed. They all seemed to be the same rotten, little rulers who would grow to be big, rotten rulers, all having kingdoms of many wives and children whom they would never hug.

I decided that I could never allow a man to rule over me. Then I wondered if the man I was to marry could still come for me. The blurry circles I stirred in the dumboy made me think more. If Father no longer owned me, and if the ugly man hadn't already given Father two pigs, one goat, and four chickens, then how could that man own me? I belonged to Mother Stevens now, and she would not sell me, would she? There were times she might. But Father hadn't told her about me being sold when he gave me away.

An old woman hissed at me. I had stopped stirring the dumboy. I moved the dough faster to cool it. I no longer cared that I was with the old women. The thought of being free from marriage made me happy for the first time since Father had given me away to Mother Stevens.

I finished the dumboy just after sunset. The men and the boys with scars had finished eating and were now drinking palm wine. They painted their faces white, made white circles around their nipples, then ran white stripes down their arms. At last, they tied strips of ribbons on their wrists.

More men than I could see to count started the fire. It was that big around at the bottom of this huge pile of wood, which had something of a point at the top. The strongest men had thrown heavy limbs high in the air to make this point.

At first, thick, white smoke appeared along with a crackling that was louder than everyone's shouts of joy. Then we all became quiet. Angry yellow flames struck high into the black sky, taller than lightening, making me fear the stars would melt.

Soon, the men and boys, acting fearless, began to dance around the fire, but not too close because it was very hot. They sang and grunted as the drums pounded rhythms, some familiar to me and some new.

Mother Stevens wanted to leave. She did not want to witness "drunken heathens" as they "desecrated," whatever that meant, the land she had prayed over to build her mission. She seemed less happy with the drums that forced their heavy poundings into our heads. At one point, she shifted her hands, which she had had clasped in prayer, to cover her ears to block the noise of the drums, my music of the bush. I begged Mother Stevens to allow me to stay. The women and girls' turn for eating was about to start.

"No. Absolutely not! Randy will drive us home," she said, as if there were something very wrong with me to ask. I complained more, telling her that these were people just like my people and that I would be safe here. Oh, the face she put in my face almost caused me to pee in the panties that Mother Stevens made me wear. I was silent after the look that ruled over me.

Mother Stevens's house had not been completed, so we left for the Missionary House in Monrovia in the new white van she had bought with the money people in America had given her, wherever America was.

She jerked my arm and nearly dragged me to the van. I stood behind the rear seat and pushed my nose against the glass of the back window, swaying to the sound of the fading drums. I gazed to the black sky at the streak of yellow fire that shot up to where Heaven was supposed to be. I wondered if God liked drums, and if he swayed with them like me. I also wondered if Mother Stevens might be right, perhaps he was offended by man's thunder.

I stayed clear of Mother Stevens after we returned to the Missionary House. I helped Mrs. Abkey in the kitchen. She was cleaning up from evening dinner, scrubbing the big roasting pan where potatoes and carrots had browned the sides. She offered to reheat the leftovers, but I was too hungry to care. Warm food was not important in the bush.

As I ate strings of tender cow meat, I listened to the rumbling pipes of Mother Stevens's tub. The pipes quieted. I imagined her slipping into the water. I had time to finish my dinner and have seconds before she would call for me to use her water for my bath. Mrs. Abkey had made a chocolate-mayonnaise cake that she flavored with coffee. I ate as fast as I could without Mrs. Abkey scolding me. I kept one eye on her and the other on my dinner plate and the hunk of cake that waited.

Once I was out of the tub, I knew that Mother Stevens would want me to spend less time massaging her feet and more time on her temples and forehead. She seemed frustrated with her robe, because it had a rip in the side seam. The humidity made her body wet with sweat. "What I would give for air-conditioning right now," she said.

Her twisted mood had tightened the muscles of her face. I preferred to rub her feet. Being too close to where her words came out made me fearful that she might become upset about something I had done but she had forgotten. Sometimes beatings came after she had relaxed, thinking about the day and remembering what I had done wrong.

# 31
# The Devil's Only Friends

I continued my massages for Mother Stevens, more so after we had moved from the Missionary House to her newly constructed home at her recently built mission. I well remember this time soon after my thirteenth rice harvest. The Bassa tribe had needed help driving the birds, and I was glad to work with them.

At Mother Stevens's mission, life expanded rapidly, because the boys kept coming and coming and coming. I was the only girl, besides Mother Stevens, at the mission.

I spent even more time rubbing Mother Stevens's feet and head before she could fall asleep. Though she would never admit it, I suspected that the quietness and the sudden strange noises of the bush upset her. I knew that the snake she had found under her suitcase had made her more anxious about living in the bush.

Now nothing sat on the floor in her room, except her white pot. I tried to explain that the snakes' nests had been destroyed when the land had been cleared for her mission. Mother Stevens said serpents were the devil's only friends.

In the evenings, I took her pot from her room to the outhouse. I tried not to look at the pot's contents as it sloshed around, brown poo mixing with yellow pee. It was impossible to avoid the odor. I relieved myself in the bush because the boys peed all over the seats.

I stopped at the opening of the outhouse. The hot sun had set behind the trees, and the cool breath of the bush drifted in a pleasing way across my arms and face. I lifted my left leg and used my toes to scratch a bug bite on my other leg. I knew what I would find inside, and I wondered if, by now, they too knew what to expect when I opened the door.

After I finished scratching, I balanced on my right foot and used a cautious toe to creak open the door. I was glad for the noise, alerting them to my presence. Their lazy eyes would look to see who dared to enter their resting place. I had been dumping Mother Stevens's pot in the bush, but someone had told on me. Mother Stevens whipped me with her electrical cord.

"Hello, I need to come in."

I eased the door open, a little wider with each nervous breath. The walls on the sides didn't go to the top, allowing the gray light of dusk to reveal a coiled mass of serpents, the same animals that had spoken to Eve in the Garden of Eden. It was their fault man must toil and women suffer labor pains. But Father hadn't toiled as far as I could tell. He worked with papers.

"Though I walk through the valley of the shadow of death, I will fear no evil, for thou art with me." I prayed for the power of God to protect me from an evil I had never known before but now feared.

I entered, ducking my head, as the snakes hung directly above me. Seeing or sensing me, they began to flow in no discernible direction.

I poured out the contents and heard the plop. I turned to flee, but one snake hung low in front of me. It stuck out its tongue like in the painting of the serpent with Eve in the Garden of Eden. I screamed and swished past its tongue-flicking face, coming only inches from its big head. I fell to my knees. Mother Stevens's pot rolled and hit a rock with a clink. I cried out for a moment, hushing quickly. I was afraid to disturb Mother Stevens.

Looking back, I saw that I had left the door open, and two ropelike serpents were dangling low. I shuddered, scrambled to retrieve the pot, then raced to the stream that flowed at the bottom of the mission property. I waded into the middle seeking protection; at least, from those snakes that didn't like the water. A big yellow moon had risen and looked at me through the trees.

I wondered if Zena and Grandma Crowcoco were on their knees praying, but I decided it was too early. They would wait until the moon had moved to the middle of the sky. I submerged the pot and brought it to the surface to dump out the water. I filled it with handfuls of sand on the second rinse then scrubbed the sides and bottom with my left hand.

"Sister?"

I jumped higher than a tomato plant, then fell over, nearly going under water. A young boy stomped in and grabbed Mother Stevens's pot before it could float downstream. I stood. He handed me the pot.

"Sorry, Sister, for scaring you."

"You didn't. I thought you were a snake," I said. I stooped over and gave the pot another rinse.

"Snake?"

"Never mind. Why are you awake? You should be sleeping."

"I'm hungry, Sister."

I realized that I too was hungry and very tired. I had worked all day, up before the sun, cooking, cleaning, and meeting everyone else's needs but mine. "Come with me." I took his hand and led him to Mother Stevens's house. "Wait here." I entered without waking her and placed the pot by her bed. Outside again, he held my hand. He was shaking.

I sat him on a log. I made a fire to heat water to make a small pot of rice. As the water boiled, I sat next to him. He was no older than eight rice fields. I placed my arm around him and sang quiet songs. He filled in the words of those refrains that he knew with a wavering voice, which was very off key.

When the rice was ready to eat, I gave him the larger portion. I left the scorched stuff on the bottom for him if he should want it. Often, all I had to eat were scrapings. The horde of boys was often more hungry than my biggest pot. Many times, boys like this one would come and want more, leaving me with nothing but the smell of rice.

The boy fell asleep next to me. I gently lowered his head, which had been resting on my thigh, to the ground. He curled on his side. I scraped the rice pot clean while watching him sleep peacefully with a full stomach.

I wasn't much larger than he was, but I picked him up and carried his sagging body to the large dormitory where the boys had cots.

The sound of two hundred sleeping boys—snoring, mumbling, coughing, and moaning—made me glad that I slept in Mother Stevens's house and that I had my own room. I didn't find an empty cot, so I laid him on the floor in a place where no one could walk on him. I said a prayer for all of them—that they would not feel as lonesome as I did. I stepped quietly up the porch steps to Mother Stevens's house, hoping she had not awakened and found me gone.

The next day, I woke very early as I always did and went to the supply hut where the cool air held the smell of oats, wheat, and rice mixed into a single, new fragrance.

On my knees in the near dark, I took a quick look overhead for snakes. Those on the ground didn't concern me. They would strike only if they were disturbed. I prayed for Zena, Mother Holmes, Mrs. Abkey, and Grandma Crowcoco, for their health and happiness. I wanted them to be happy, even though I was not. I prayed for the boys that I would have enough oats in my biggest pot to feed them and prayed for strength to carry the pot to the dining area after it had cooled.

I had fallen into the pot once, some time ago. Luckily, it had not been filled with boiling water or steaming rice. I had grown stronger, and now I could lift the pot without dragging it or falling in. I had already hurt my back before Randy showed me how to use my legs to lift. Zena had never carried such heavy objects, or she would have shown me how to lift without hurting myself.

I prayed Mother Stevens would adopt another daughter, who was bigger and older than me, to help. I knew she would not hire cooks, as Mother Holmes did, to tend to the boys. A mouse's prickly feet ran across my calves, momentarily startling me.

I prayed Randy would do badly in school, so he would have to help me. Then I felt terrible for wishing him misfortune. I prayed for him to receive his due treasure in Heaven, which I knew was not the Christian thing to pray for, because Randy was a thief and a liar. He always blamed me for things that were missing, and I got his beatings.

I placed my hands on the floor and bowed, trying to stretch the pain in my back. I needed to cry but was afraid I would not stop if I started.

"What are you doing?" Mother Stevens demanded.

I jumped up and said, "Nothing, ma'am." Then added, "Getting oats for breakfast." Doing nothing would result in a whipping, I feared.

"Then stop wasting time. The children will be up soon."

She turned and left. I poked out my tongue. I wanted to swear like some of the boys did when they talked among themselves.

# 32
# Sealed Plastic Tub

Mother Stevens had purchased plastic storage containers with tight-fitting lids that made it easier to keep her rice and oats free of the weevils, at least most of them, that were abundant in the storeroom's meals and grains. Once, she found a lid off, and I got a whipping.

It began to rain. I filled the bucket with the oats that I would boil for breakfast. A river flowed from the sky, creating instant streams and huge puddles. I sloshed to the covered area where my big black pots waited for their fire. I set the dry oats next to the pots.

There were no coals to start the palm fibers and splintered wood, plus they were damp, as were my matches. Match after match I wasted. I became so frustrated, I began to speak in tongues, a language even God could not understand. Still no fire. I kept trying. I had to feed the boys who had begun to gather around me to tell me how to make a fire, as if they knew better than me.

I started to curse the rain under my breath, not swearing, then gave up. The sky was gray-blue, telling me of the sun rising behind the rain clouds.

I looked to Mother Stevens's house. Lights glowed from her window. I had to start the fire. I ran to the storage hut, knowing what I would do. What I had to do.

I grabbed one of Mother Stevens's special plastic tubs and dumped her weevil-free oats into a large empty sack. Then I used a knife to shred an old, dry sack into ribbons, stuffing the ribbons into the container. When it was full, I sealed the lid and ran back to the cooking area. It worked. The dry sackcloth ignited easily, and it overpowered the moist hair of the palm tree, setting it on fire in blue and orange flames. I waited a few moments, then added the splintered wood, waited a bit more, then added larger pieces on the growing fire.

The big pot began to warm. I ran to the well, back and forth, until I finally had enough water to cook the oats. I added more wood under the pot. The growing fire was so hot, the damp wood steamed for only moments before it broke into flames. Mrs. Abkey had shown me how to wait until the water was boiling to add the oats to the water. It made them less mushy.

I shook the meal into the angry, boiling water to prevent lumps. Steam dampened my hands and climbed my arms. Eye-rubbing boys gathered. One grasped the wooden paddle and began to gently stir. How he knew to do this I didn't know, but when I finished adding the oats, I took the paddle from him. I enjoyed watching the hypnotic eddies, like those I used to watch in the river from the monkey bridge.

"Jeanette!"

My heart leapt to the bottom of my throat and plugged my breath.

Mother Stevens stood over me. Her eyes were narrow slits. She had mud on her bare feet. She was never outside without her shoes and never in the rain without her umbrella.

Perhaps it was my look of surprise that made her point to her special container; then I understood what had brought her out in the rain and mud. The lid was off, and through the clear bottom it appeared as if mud was inside. Excuses were no shield from punishment. She would punish me. She knew it. I knew it.

The boys around me stood straight, as if they were a group of black spears, perhaps fearing they were also guilty because they stood close to me.

"Now *you* must wash my feet." Her eyes were wide open, daring me to defy her. She turned and stomped back to her house, making tracks that I would have to clean.

"Why don't you run away?" an older boy said. He was tall and skinny and had a large boil on his cheek next to his flat nose. "Go back to your tribe." He seemed sincere, but I was uncertain if he was trying to be mean or helpful. "But you are so flat chested that no man would want you." He reached for my chest to touch me where my breasts would be if I'd had them. I backed away before he could make contact. I pulled the paddle from the oats and threatened to hit him.

He laughed and headed toward the tables where the other boys sat and waited.

I continued to hold the paddle in front of me. Thick globs clung near the end. A small boy focused intently with cupped hands to catch anything that might slip off. I pulled the paddle toward me. His hands followed. I reached for the sand-colored meal, extended my finger, then scraped the oats into his hands.

His intense eyes thanked me. He blew on the steaming pile and gobbled it as quickly as his mouth would tolerate the heat. He seemed satisfied for a moment, but I knew this partial serving would only make him hungrier.

Soon, the boys formed a line. The larger ones shoved the smaller ones to the side. Those smaller ones squeezed in where *they* were bigger. I enjoyed fulfilling the word of God, "The first shall be last and the last shall be first." Once I began scooping, I scooped smaller portions for the taller boys who were in front, saving more for those who were last. This gave me great satisfaction. I didn't stop serving until every bowl had been filled.

As the boys held out their bowls, I examined them for remnants of oats. I had learned that clever boys would use their fingers and tongues to wipe the bowls clean and get back in line.

If I suspected deceit, I looked at the boys' lips and the edges of their mouths for evidence of first helpings. If they were smiling, I observed the spaces between their teeth for oats. I would also check their height in line. If I had just served a short boy and a taller one was next, then I became very suspicious.

I also watched out for those seeking seconds because I wanted enough left for me. Often, I was left with the scorched scraping at the bottom. This was the case today.

After the boys had scurried to their classroom building and after the rain left the sky, I cleaned up. I peeled away any remnants of food from the big, black kettles. I didn't waste the paper-thin scum that had formed around the sides. I ate it.

I washed two hundred bowls and the spoons that Mother Stevens had insisted on, even though we would have been happy to use our fingers. I washed and rinsed in big silver tubs of soap and cold water, placing the bowls and spoons on green, rubber-coated racks to dry.

I hummed as I washed. I tilted my head down, looking at the white, bubbly suds, then looked up at the morning sky and its flock of white clouds, wondering if they were also made of soap. The birds in the trees—parrots—took flight. I listened to the squawking birds that created a noise so loud that I wanted to hold my soapy hands over my ears. I watched them circle. Something had driven them away from where they were resting.

The sun glimmered flashes of green and yellow from their outstretched wings, gliding, twisting side to side, making me dizzy with their circles, until they landed back in the treetops from which they had come.

I quickly finished the dishes. I knew Mother Stevens would want her house cleaned before I cleaned the boys' dorm, which I hated because it smelled of body odor and moldy clothes. They didn't use limes under their arms like Zena and me, when I remembered to use them.

I walked slowly to Mother Stevens's house. I didn't know if she would be there or not. Teachers taught the boys their ABCs and higher levels of learning. None of the teachers were as nice as Miss Johnson. They came from Monrovia or nearby villages, where people who had money lived. Some even taught their own sons.

Mother Stevens waited somewhere. Perhaps at her desk that sat in the corner of her living room. She took a lot of time writing letters to those who sent her money. She had done this for hours and hours at the Missionary House. Mrs. Abkey had told me that it takes a lot of charity from others who have love in their hearts for the poor African children to run a mission. They must have given generously to Mother Stevens's mission, because there was always food coming in on trucks.

Zena and I had also been poor, and if Father had not given us the fifty cents when I ran up to him, then we would have had only rice and vegetables to eat. But we were happy. We hadn't had to write letters asking for help. We did need Father, an acceptance that hadn't come easily to me.

Mother Stevens stood waiting inside the front door. She held the electrical cord in her right hand. I looked back at the special container that still sat in the mud. I scraped my feet on the bristle mat, then noticed the muddy footprints she had made on the floor.

As with Father and now with Mother Stevens, acceptance was best. Expressions of gratitude were better. Mother Stevens prayed for me as she swatted my back, bottom, and legs. I had often wondered why Miss Johnson hadn't beaten her schoolchildren to get us to be better behaved in her class.

I cleaned the mud tracks she had made and also cleaned the special box for her rice. I cut open a newer bag of rice and took out a handful at a time, dropping the grains in a flat pan and shaking it to separate the grains. This made it easier to pick out the weevils. After each weevil inspection and removal, I dumped the cleaned rice into Mother Stevens's special container.

The new welts on my back and bottom and legs burned as I worked, feeling as if I were standing too close to a fire. In the relative cool of the storage area, I took my time, sorting worms from rice.

# 33
# Miss Palmer

For the first year, I cooked and cleaned up after the boys and Mother Stevens. Time passed dreadfully slowly. Each day of toil seemed longer. Each morning it was more difficult to put my tired feet to the floor, until I thought about my time alone with God. My morning devotions sustained my spirit throughout the day. The storage hut became my chapel, where I prayed to God and sang songs to the rafters. But my body had grown weary from the hard work that repeated every day for months and months and months.

The summer rain came as a great relief. Parents came to get their sons and take them home. Each day I found time to play. I ran to the swing, which was similar to the one Mother Holmes had, and waited for the tall man and short woman. I would stay for as long as I could. Often, I remained too long. Mother Stevens would call for me in her sharp voice when she needed something.

This wet summer and the next long, dry, winter of school gave the same result: too much work, too many boys, and too much time spent longing for

Zena and Father to come and take me home.

After all of the boys were gone, Mother Stevens occasionally retreated to the Missionary House in Monrovia. I would accompany her, but sometimes she left me alone at the mission to do extra work: scrubbing the floors of the storage hut, classrooms, and dorm and deep cleaning the bathing areas, where the boys played more than they bathed.

Once I was done with my chores at the mission, I joined Mother Stevens in Monrovia, where there were more sidewalks and less mud.

One day, we walked in the rain; rather, I walked in the rain while Mother Stevens hid under a black umbrella. She kept fussing with its position, looking down at me. I was not certain what she was more concerned about: my new white dress, heavy with rain, which dragged on the sidewalk and caused the ruffles on the hem to become brown with dirt, or me.

Fearful she would blame me for the rain, I tugged at the dress that clung to me like a snake's skin to its body. I remained mindful to keep pace with her fast and determined steps. Her shoes began to slosh and make squeaking noises. Annoyed, I thought, she kicked them off and walked in her bare feet, like me. This was the only time I felt I had something in common with her. Mother Stevens left her shoes for me to pick up.

We stopped in front of the First National Bank of Liberia. The rain pounded on the metal roof above our heads and made it impossible for me to hear what Mother Stevens was saying. I nodded an acknowledgement of understanding and felt safe doing so. I had been in the bank with her before. I knew what she expected of me—invisibility.

She put her umbrella next to others, adding to the mushroom-field appearance. I set her shoes down. She slipped into them. She looked me over. She shook her head, apparently, for what she didn't see in me. I looked at my soggy reflection in the dark window and compared it to Mother Stevens, who was mostly dry. She was tall and had the fullness of a woman. I wondered if I would ever have a womanly shape. My chest, where my breasts might someday be, was as flat as my stomach. With my pencil appearance, I might have been another stray boy who had come out of the bush into the city. I had lived fourteen rice fields and wondered how many more it would be before I became a woman. Zena had lived fourteen rice fields when she had borne me and had no breasts to feed me.

Mother Stevens gripped the door handle and pulled open the large glass door. The air inside was cool and full of the smell of paper and ink, which made me breathe in deeply. She went ahead, and I scurried with tangled feet to keep close. She used her softest voice to greet those who met her. They called her "Miss Stevens."

Mother Stevens seemed to know where to go. She walked toward a man in a dark-blue suit, who stood up from behind his desk. He reached out his hand, smiled big and wide, then shook Mother Stevens's hand. Her posture softened, tilting her head to the side as if she were shy. She cleared her throat and cooed his name. She didn't sit. He hurried from around his desk and pulled her chair out. Mother Stevens sat. She scooted closer, placing her bent arms on top of the desk. He scurried back, sat in his big leather chair, and moved papers to give her arms more room. He raised his hand. I turned to see why he was signaling.

The most beautiful woman I had ever seen, even prettier than Miss Johnson, my former teacher, stood across the big room from us. She looked at me, smiling, making me think she might even like me. She swayed toward me. Her hips moved like none I had ever seen before. She stopped at a table and pulled tissues from a box, then started in my direction again. I might have been in trouble, but she kept smiling and gliding with the smooth motion of a long-winged hawk. Her short black skirt exposed graceful legs, and her white blouse, which was unbuttoned more than Mother Stevens would ever have done, bulged with breasts that were the largest I had ever seen.

I let out a deep breath.

She knelt before me. "What is your name, pretty girl?"

She took the wad of tissues and dabbed my face. She smiled again. Her teeth glimmered, the whitest white against her smooth skin, which was a light shade of black. Her brown eyes had flecks of gold in them.

"Jabonkah," I said, forgetting my English name. I wanted to be like her: confident, beautiful, kind, and wearing a pretty, pleated dress.

"You poor thing, you're soaked to the bone." She turned me and wiped the back of my neck, then rotated me again and said, "I'm Miss Palmer. And we are best friends now, Jabonkah."

I could not see Mother Stevens, but heard her say, "Jeanette, that's Jeanette *Stevens*." Mother Stevens claimed me like she might claim the umbrella she had left at the entrance.

"Oh, then, Jeanette, you're a most fortunate girl to be *Miss* Stevens's daughter."

I turned to look at Mother Stevens. I loved Miss Palmer. Mother Stevens straightened in her chair and said to the man, "Jeffery, I'm a very busy woman. Can we get on with business?" Miss Palmer seemed to irritate Mother Stevens, and that filled me with a sense of joy.

"Let's go to the bathroom, sweetheart," Miss Palmer said, still squatting. "We must tend to you properly." She stood and took my hand. I wanted to hug her. I wanted to be her daughter. I looked back to see if Mother Stevens was watching. She was not. I wanted her to. I wanted her to see that Miss Palmer could be nice to me, seemed to even like me. But Mother Stevens would not look at me—not even if God were to fill this room with thunder, I suspected.

# 34
# Turn to Rust

Randy was eighteen, older than me by four rice fields. He was tall, handsome, black as a moonless night, and not to be trusted. I had decided Mother Stevens only had enough love for one person, so she had given it to Randy. He went to the best school in Monrovia, and she bought him new clothes and a wristwatch, which seemed like a stupid thing to wear when the sun could tell you the time. He never helped me with the boys or my other chores. He would have had me wait on him, but I refused.

It was just before the boys returned for another year, my third, that Mother Stevens, Randy, and I were alone at the mission.

The rainy season had passed. The ground was dry. Some schools met during the rains; however, Mother Stevens couldn't tolerate mud and dirty boys. I was in agreement with her. I disliked boys, well, most of them, muddy or not.

While Mother Stevens was writing letters in her room, Randy had taken the white van to Monrovia to buy things she wanted. If I could have reached the pedals in the van, I would have been the one who went to Monrovia instead of lazy Randy. He was expected to return in the afternoon.

I was alone in the great expanse of the mission, walking softly, moving as if I were not trying to catch a rooster for our dinner, which I was. I had my eye on one that was not too old and not too young. The old ones knew, or suspected, what I had in mind, so I ignored them for now. But, one day, they would become too complacent. The young ones didn't have enough meat on their bones for the three of us.

I carried a special bucket full of weevil-infested rice, which I didn't keep in the storage hut. I continued to walk slowly, careful not to reveal my murderous intent. Although I could run, dodge, and burrow into the tiniest places a chicken might hide, it was easier to catch them in the open after cornering them.

I scattered the grain and worms near the long side of the boys' dormitory, where I had previously plugged the big holes that a scared chicken could squeeze through. I waited for the chickens to gather. I sat on my heels. They were clucking and bobbing their heads as they do, keeping one eye on the ground and one on me. I knew the bird I wanted. He was a fighter and was mean to the hens, always trying to mount them. He had a torn spur claw that dangled on his left leg.

I hummed Zena's song. While I remained sitting, I shuffled closer to the rooster with the torn claw. He was suspicious. I had chased him before, and he must have remembered me throwing my bucket at him in frustration. But this time, I waited until he had scattered the hens and the young roosters from the grain I tossed. The old ones just ate. My rooster of interest kept pecking closer to where I tossed less and less grain and weevils.

His red eyes were alert. He pecked, looked at me, then pecked again at the weevils. He had to be happy to have so many weevils, but, still, he must have suspected danger. There was no way he could know that I was going to clobber him instead of chase him.

I had a rock the size of my fist in my bucket. I was a keen shot with rocks, having developed my aim from my love of butter pears. The limbs were too small to climb, so I had become good at knocking down the high-hanging ones with mud clods.

My rock would not kill him, unless I hit him on the head. I only needed to slow him down so I could pounce on him. I waited and waited and waited until he seemed more concerned with eating. After a while, he became very excited about the handfuls of wormy rice I dumped close to me.

His pecking rhythm became increasingly intense. I drifted to the right. Maybe he thought I was giving him more space, but I was placing him between me and the corner, where the bush consisted of thick thorns, a place he would not burrow into to escape.

It was time. My stomach was both excited for the chase and hungry for the taste of chicken. My throwing hand was wet with sweat. The rice and weevils clung to it. I gathered the rock in my left hand. I rotated its position until it fit solidly in my palm. An inner chill ran down my spine as the impulse to throw the stone grew stronger. Still, I waited for the next time he ducked and exposed the back of his head.

I jumped and threw the rock hard and fast, hitting him on the side of the neck. I didn't remember dropping the bucket. Seeing him on his side, flapping like he wanted to fly into the ground, caused me to holler, "I got him!" I flung my body and scooped in his wings and held him tight. I quickly freed my left hand to grab his flailing legs and dangerous claws.

He pounded his head against the red earth and cried the most awful squawk, which caused me to momentarily pause with pity, until I had heard enough and stood, holding him upside down by his legs. I let him fan my face with the air from his flapping wings. He was mine. His cries hurt my ears, so I did what Zena had taught me—I laid him over on his back in my open hands. He calmed and became quiet, blinking at me, not knowing what was coming next, and you never let the other chickens see you remove the head of one of their own.

Behind the storage hut, where no one ever goes, not even the chickens, I draped his head over a log. I felt some sadness as he looked up at me. I swung the machete, fast and clean. Blood squirted out in an arch like a boy peeing. I flipped his headless body upside-down in the air with one hand. I started pulling the soft feathers from around his legs while I let the last of his blood drip. After he had bled out, I lit the wood under a small pot that I had filled with palm oil. I plucked him clean and gutted him, saving his heart, gizzard, and liver. The oil began to smoke, my clue to know the oil was hot enough to fry. I gently lowered his body into the bubbling oil. It erupted with angry, golden bubbles that swarmed the surface with splattering and crackling.

The aromas created saliva that rolled over my bottom lip before I could close my mouth. I shut my eyes. The rising steam dampened my face.

Someone poked me in the back. I jumped.

"What are you cooking?" Randy said. He placed his hand on my shoulder and moved me to the side. He leaned over the pot. "Look at the size of those drumsticks! Those are mine." He gazed at me, as if I were a rain cloud that would soon pass by.

*I wanted the drumsticks.*

"How much longer?" he said.

The bird was almost done. "Oh, a long time," I lied. He had colas in a brown paper bag; they had made the bottom and sides of the bag wet. Mother Stevens liked her colas cool, so I knew he could not stay and bother me for long.

"You're lying." Now he looked at me, as if I were a bug on his skin that he was about to swat. "I want those legs." He shoved me in the chest. "Besides, if you eat what is not yours, you'll turn to rust inside."

I shook my head. I knew he was trying to scare me. "Leave me alone." I grabbed several sticks of wood, thought about throwing them at him, then placed them on the fire.

He walked toward Mother Stevens's house, paused for a moment, then raised his fist at me. He shook it and continued to shake it while walking to Mother Stevens's house.

The chicken was done. So when Randy was out of sight, I scooped the crispy bird from the oil with a strong metal screen that had a wooden handle, like one Father had made for Zena, and put the rooster in a serving bowl. I was hungry and angry. I gathered a smaller bowl. I broke off both chicken legs with quick fingers, nearly burning them in my need to hurry. The steaming meat nearly fell from the bone as I transferred the legs into my bowl. I took the lid off a pot that contained leftover rice and buried the legs under the rice, like a dog hiding his bones.

I ran to the storage hut. I sat on a rice bag and ate both legs and the oil-soaked rice. I lay back with a happy stomach and looked up at the same ceiling that listened to my morning prayers. A loud grumbling noise came from my middle. I tried to force a burp. None came.

"Jeanette!" It was Mother Stevens's cutting voice, opening me up, allowing more guilt to flood in and probably turning my insides to rust, according to Randy. I knew what was in store for me by Mother Stevens's tone.

I woke to a dark morning. My stomach was cramped and my back stung from the beating Mother Stevens had given me for eating Randy's drumsticks.

Last night, I had crept out of Mother Stevens's house, careful not to wake her or Randy. I walked to the storage hut where I knelt and prayed for forgiveness for being a liar and a glutton. I didn't know what a glutton was, but I was sure God did. Mother Stevens had said that word over and over until I formed a sickening dislike for it. I unlocked my prayerful hands and used them to press against my aching stomach. The harder I pushed the better I felt. I curled into a lump and soon fell asleep again.

Slits of sunlight forced their way into the storage room. I had overslept, but the mission was quiet. I listened carefully, finally remembering that the boys had not yet arrived. I sat up, then stood, stretching and yawning.

I looked down at the white rice sack I had lain on and saw red. I spread my legs and looked down. Rust! It had stained the insides of my legs. "Randy!" Why I screamed out his name, I was not certain, but I screamed and screamed and screamed for Randy, until the door flew open and he ran in.

"What's wrong?"

"Randy! Look, I'm rusted." I pointed to the sack, then to my legs, opening them so he could see.

His roaring laughter pained my ears and hurt my feelings. He bent in hideous enjoyment of my terrible misfortune, all because I had eaten his chicken legs. I switched from great fear to pure anger and pounded on his back. "You cursed me. I'm dying!"

Randy grabbed me and slapped his hand over my mouth "Oh, shut up, you stupid girl."

Mother Stevens, still wearing her robe, hurried in. "What on earth is the matter?"

"The dummy started her period," Randy said.

Now my hatred for Randy was as big as the sky. Of course I knew that women bled from where our legs grow from our bodies, but it had never happened to me, and Zena had never told me it would.

# 35
# Grab Her Now

Soon after my first period, other changes began to take place, and these changes didn't go unnoticed by a school full of boys. They had always teased me that I just pretended to be a girl; mostly, I thought, because I could outrun, out climb, out jump, and out fish all of them. But the true reason, I now suspected, was because I was flat chested at fourteen rice fields. Once, a few boys had followed me into the bush, hoping to get a glimpse under my dress when I poo. (The snakes still owned the outhouse.)

But during the year of my fifteenth rice field, my breasts grew and grew and grew, until my dress no longer lay flat against my stomach. At first, when the boys had come back to school, they accused me of tying halves of oranges to my chest. Those same boys attempted to touch me. They were also older and had hair under their arms.

Hands continued to dart at me from the sides and even from behind. But I was too quick and chopped them away before they touched me. I wanted to complain to Mother Stevens but feared she would make it *my* fault and then whip me.

I still toiled while everyone else played, studied, taught, or wrote letters asking for money. I had grown an inch or two taller from when Mother Stevens had adopted me. During my first year, I had damaged my back by lifting the heavy cooking pot, and it had never gotten better. Somehow my spine hurt more with each passing year.

Pain was a given: in my body, in my heart, in my spirit, longing for God to free me from slavery. I had heard the Bible story of Jacob who was forced by Laban to work in slavery for years for his true love Rachel, but my forced labor had no goal or reward except more pain.

My knees should be flat, I spent so much time praying to God to take me to Heaven to be with him, to free me from my misery. I was in continual communication with God, but felt as if he were tired of listening to my same prayers.

One time, I tried to keep my eyes closed, but they kept popping open, even though I was exhausted and weary from head to foot. I wanted someone to rub me like I did Mother Stevens, each night, until she fell asleep. The crickets and the frogs were challenging each other to see which could annoy me the most. My bug bites, which had not bothered me during the day, itched intolerably. I considered stripping and scraping my skin against a banana tree.

Then I heard giggling from outside. Some boys were up to something. I sniffed the air. I had not bathed recently. Jasmine was in bloom. I thought I smelled boys nearby, but it could have been my memory of them. I hated the smell of boys, oily-sour hair and rotten underarms. It was everywhere.

"Hey, Jeanette."

Snickering. What were they thinking? They would wake Mother Stevens.

"We need to talk." Stifled laughter. "And we—" That voice was cut off.

I knew them. The older boys, my age. I wondered how many.

"Go away," I whispered. "I'll beat you."

"We have something for you," the stronger voice said.

"I don't want it," I said, but I wondered if they really had something.

"It came from Bomi Hills."

"That's a—" I hushed myself. I was too loud. They were lying. I waited. They waited. I began to wonder about Zena. Was she okay? "Is it a letter?"

"Yes!"

"Who's it from?"

They paused.

"Quick, tell me, or I'll come and beat both of you."

"It's too dark…you come look."

I sat up, still undecided. Zena could not write, but what if someone had done it for her? Even through her closed door, I could hear Mother Stevens breathing heavily. Her nose was plugged from the wild flowers that were in bloom, especially the jasmine. I had to know if they had news about Zena. The crickets in my room hushed when I got out of bed. I crept out of the house on my toes.

The two older boys had a smaller boy behind them. The smaller one was nice. Why he came with them puzzled me. The two older boys ruled the others. They stood tall, and the moonlight made their white T-shirts glow, a whiteness that reminded me of my father's shirts. I didn't have to search long to find the buckets of angry thoughts I kept for him.

I knew there was no letter. Zena could not write nor did she know how to locate me. I hated these boys for creating hope that I might learn something about Zena. My anger grew with each step I took. The fight was on. I was ready to beat them, bloody their noses, send them crying for their mothers. I felt my hatred build. My fists were closed so tightly, they could have crushed a stone to powder.

They grabbed the smaller boy and shoved him in between them and me. He looked frightened. I didn't care. I would pound him, too.

"He wants to have you," the taller of the two older boys said.

I glared into the little boy's eyes. He was shaking his head. They shoved him into me. "Grab her now!" He pushed off my chest, then fled toward the boy's dorm. "We'll get you later," the tallest one whisper-yelled at the running boy.

"Leave me alone, or I'll beat both of you."

They looked at each other, then back at me.

"No," the taller said.

"Last chance," I said, then I tried to stretch to their height. They were both taller by a full head. I had been beaten for as long as I could remember, brutally cut in the Society, pounded in the face, and whipped with electrical cords. I knew the taste of my own blood. I was not going to let these boys have the best of me and would never allow them to touch my body.

I stepped forward. They moved to the sides, spreading apart like two dogs surrounding a rabbit.

"What are you waiting for? Cowards." I raised my fists as I had seen boys do in fights.

The shorter of the two jumped toward me, then leaped back, just as quickly. In a flash, the taller boy had me in his arms, one arm around my neck and his free hand over my mouth. The second boy restrained my hands, because I had used them to gouge my nails into the arms of the boy who choked me.

I screamed through his hands. I tried to bite him, but he pulled my head back too far. I stomped my heels, attempting to break his toes. The boy who had my arms was stronger than me, though I resisted. I flailed my head side to side. All parts of me struggled against their attack.

The hand of the boy that held my mouth slipped away from the wetness of my saliva. I bit his hand hard, as if I were biting through the toughest chicken gizzard.

"Ouch! You bush dog."

Before I could scream, he kneed me in the back, in the place that always hurt. My body went slack, stunned from the pain. The boy in front of me held my nightshirt as I fell to the ground. He slipped it over my head, exposing my chest, which they must have stared at as I looked up to the blurry stars.

They squeezed my breasts, repeatedly. They hurt them. They were breathing hard.

What I remember next was pounding the face of one of the boys. I must have grabbed one of them in a rage; which one, I didn't know or care. I beat and beat and beat him, until I was lifted into the air. It was Mother Stevens. She had pulled me away. The boys ran, but I continued to scream at them using words I didn't realize I knew but must have had heard the boys say.

"Jeanette, what have you done? What were you doing outside with them?"

"Beating them," I said, spattering my words.

She hugged me, for the first time, ever, in three years.

I was suddenly very tired. Mother Stevens walked me to my room. That was the last thing I remember of that night.

# 36
# God Spoke to Me

The intensity of my prayers increased the longer I remained in slavery at Mother Stevens's mission. I had first learned about slavery from the Bible, and also how free blacks and freed slaves had come to Liberia many years ago. I occasionally listened outside the windows of classrooms. It was true. I was a slave. Mother Stevens and her two hundred boys were my masters. I received no compensation other than Mother Stevens continually saying that we were doing the work of the Lord, and our rewards would be in Heaven. She did give me a small allowance; maybe because she was afraid of what I might do to get money from the boys or that I would steal it from them or her.

I was tired. My hands and arms were scarred from hot pots and angry fires. My joy in God's creation was gone. If I was earning my reward in Heaven, then that is where I wanted to be—in Heaven with Jesus.

I never cried when I prayed for Mrs. Abkey, Zena, Mother Holmes, Randy, and Mother Stevens. But each time I prayed for myself, I had to drive away my emotions. Tears splattered the rice bag that I used as an altar.

I begged God to take me from here to be with Jesus.

Four years of bondage had broken my spirit. Four years of being whipped made me desperate to belong to another mother who would love me, like Zena. Four years of boys made me question God's plan for mankind—why should men rule?

Running away often came to mind but dissipated quickly when I thought of Father's belt and the unforgiving bush where no one could live alone. Mother Holmes had told me that for every stray dog there were three stray children. At least I was not begging for or stealing food and had a place to sleep.

In the bush, Zena and I had lived each day. We'd never longed for a different today or for a tomorrow that might be better. We would long for a different man, whom Zena called John Henry and whom I called Father, but never for a different life. We'd had each other. We'd had each day to live and work to satisfy our simple needs.

"Jeanette!"

Mother Stevens's sharp voice sliced through the peace of the predawn like a thorn rips tender skin. Were there chores I had forgotten? Had I emptied her pot? If it were not fresh and clean in the morning, she would become angry. On the other hand, she never got up this early. Perhaps she was ill.

"Jeanette!"

She was more frustrated than her usual displeased self. She wanted something. But what?

Her voice grabbed and pulled on the sore muscles in my back. I rose from my prayers, aching as I sat up. I forced myself to stand. I left the storage hut. Leaning to my right, I ran to her, leaving the door to the storage hut open.

Mother Stevens stood in the doorway of her house. A yellow light shone behind her that made her into a dark shadow, reminding me of the devil from the Society. I slowed to a walk.

I told myself that Mama Kama had been the Society Devil, and Mother Stevens was not the devil. Still, she frightened me.

"Come. Come."

She seemed excited now. I wondered what it could be.

She gathered her robe, hurried across the porch, then walked toward me. "Jeanette," she said, seeming happy, "I had this dream...God spoke to me."

"He...did?" My mouth hung open. I was that surprised.

She grabbed both arms and drew me in for a hug. We didn't fit together as Zena and I had. She pushed me back. She looked at me as if she liked me. "Yes, he told me you were to marry Randy." She hugged me again.

I squirmed away from her, shaking my head. "Would that mean...I would have to lie with him? And he would rule over me?"

"Yes...yes, I suppose. You'd be man and wife."

I backed away from her, still shaking my head. I already washed Randy's clothes and ironed them. There was no way Randy would ever rule over me. I would never let him touch me like a wife. Then I remembered that I had been sold. "My father sold me, years ago," I said.

Darkness hid her face, so I was not able to judge her reaction. I added, "The man paid two pigs, one goat, and four chickens for me." Then I tried to remember the man who had bought me seven rice fields ago. Perhaps Randy would be a better husband—at least he was more my age. Then I blurted out. "But God didn't tell *me* I was supposed to marry Randy."

My feet rose in the air, and my arms nearly broke away from my body. Mother Stevens whisked me into the house, legs dangling, head jerking around, then stood me next to her bed.

"How dare you question God's will!" She released my arm. "Don't move."

She left me standing. I waited, knowing what was going to happen next. I worried that the fire was not yet started. The boys were waking and hungry. I breathed deeply. My back had sharp pains. I tried to relax. It hurt less if I didn't fight the pain. I wondered if God had given me the same dream he had given to Mother Stevens, I might have felt differently. Perhaps I had spoken too soon. I had always spoken too soon. Why would God talk to me? My head seemed too heavy for my neck. It fell forward. My chin touched my chest.

I thought about agreeing to marry Randy, not to stop the beating but because I was a bad girl. I knew it. Father had known it. Zena had warned me over and over and over: "Too many words, Jabonkah."

The first lash struck. I wondered if God felt the same—too many words Jabonkah; too many prayers for yourself. I grunted with the second and third whips. I prayed to God for forgiveness. I appealed to Jesus for his intercession and mercy to make me a better person so Mother Stevens would love me.

"You will never question the will of God again," she said, while she delivered the last stinging blow, this time to the backs of my bare legs in case, I suspected, my back had grown numb.

God's will was so mysterious. I wondered who could possibly know what he wanted. But I wanted him to take me to Heaven or tell me what he wanted from me or give me rest from the boys and Mother Stevens, even if it meant death. I was a bad girl. I knew it. Jesus loved all the little children, and surely Jesus knew that Liberia was part of the world, part of Africa at least.

"Now, feed the boys. You're late," Mother Stevens said, forcing her words as if through clinched teeth.

"Yes, ma'am." The pain in my back grew stronger as I straightened, pushing away from Mother Stevens's quilted bed cover. I looked on the bed cover for tear drops that might upset her.

I brushed off the top layer of ash from last night's fire. I was glad to be free of Mother Stevens's immediate control and glad to see red embers. My mind kept repeating, "Jesus loves me. Jesus loves me. Jesus loves me." My heart inflamed with sorrow as the flames grew and the wood crackled and popped, sending sparks flying in many directions.

A few boys huddled around the growing fire. One said, "Sister, you're late." They all looked at me as if agreeing with the boy who had spoken.

"Go wash your hands," I grumbled. It was still dark. Their hands might have been clean, but boys were always dirty. They didn't leave me. They remained defiant.

"No oats for you, then," I said with a growl.

I was prepared to fight. It was best if they left me. I could beat them all and still make breakfast. But I turned away. It was a man's world.

# 37
# Hungry for Sixteen Rice Fields

The smell of roses filled the room. Mother Stevens soaked in her bubble bath and hummed hymns, which were usually sung with greater tempo. I laid her pressed pajamas on her down-turned bed, straightening and smoothing them against the cool linen sheets.

"Ma'am, I'm emptying the pot now."

She paused her humming. "Be sure to wash your hands afterward."

"Yes, ma'am." I always washed my hands, and she always reminded me.

The night air was heavy with moisture. Crickets creaking, frogs croaking, and the calls of distant birds singing to me, yet I was anxious once again. The hanging snakes tested my courage. I grasped the long stick I kept beside the outhouse door. I waved it before me as I entered. The night was too dark to see if any snakes dangled close to my head.

Swoosh. Swoosh. I whipped the stick back and forth, hitting nothing. If I had hit one, giving it a solid whack, it would have recoiled and retreated higher in the rafters, hissing its resentment.

With the pot empty, I stopped at the new station Mother Stevens had

had a man build where I could scrub her pot without going to the river. I did the final rinse, washed my hands, then returned the clean pot to her room. I made certain to place the pot in the exact spot where Mother Stevens could find it even on the darkest nights. My hands smelled of Lava soap. Often, she sniffed them to check if they were clean.

I turned out the lights. Her shadow poked into the room through the crack in the bathroom door; its dark presence moved with her motions as she toweled her body.

"Turn the fan on," Mother Stevens said.

I went to the wall and pushed the switch up for the ceiling fan, which hung above her bed. It slowly came to life.

I had seen Mother Stevens naked. My hands had discovered everything there was to know: how many moles she had and one that sprouted curls; how the coarseness of the hair on her legs changed, becoming smoother from her ankles to her hips; how the stiff wire in her bras made grooves under each of her breasts. Her private parts were hers alone as mine were to me. But I was curious to know how a woman looked who had not suffered the cutting of the Society.

And now, as a woman of sixteen rice fields, I wondered what sensations had been taken away from my body. I would never know pleasure from a man, if there was any.

At first, Mother Stevens had told me to look away when she came from the bathroom. Zena and I had never been protective of being seen by each other, except for that one time when I'd asked her to spread her legs. Now, after four years, Mother Stevens was at ease as she walked naked into the dark room to her bed where her pajamas waited for her.

She needed extra light to dress. She had left the bathroom light on and the door open. Steam clung to the mirror. After she had dressed, I narrowed the opening. She lay on top of the sheets, and the springs of the bed squeaked and complained as she got comfortable, settling on her stomach. She moaned and released a long breath. She spread her arms and legs apart and waited for me to begin.

The rainy season was over. The ground had dried and so had the shins of Mother Stevens's legs. Liberia's tropical moisture kept the rest of her skin supple and smooth.

With her face pressed into the mattress, she mumbled, "Don't forget the balls." I had forgotten once. Now she reminded me each time I rubbed her feet. I cupped and squeezed the ball of her right foot. Until hers, I had never felt smooth feet.

I wondered if the things I had forgotten had caused me to receive so many beatings from Father and now from Mother Stevens.

I started to rub her left foot, and I was reminded of my left handedness. I recalled a verse about plucking out your offending eye, because it was better to have only one than to go to Hell. Once I had learned to read, I hadn't found anything in the Bible about an offending left hand but came to realize that you could substitute an eye for a hand.

"Stop daydreaming." Mother sounded upset. I moved quickly to the side of her bed and began rubbing the calf of her left leg, hard and deep, as she liked it. The effort soon made beads of sweat appear on my forehead. Although she had dried herself, her skin was wet. The moving air from the fan helped, and she was drier than before, but her pajamas still clung to her.

I feared she might feel my drops of sweat fall on her legs; she had in the past. It meant additional trouble I didn't need. I felt the weight of each new irritation I caused Mother Stevens, each added to my self-loathing, and each I placed on top of a huge bundle that carried on my head like cassava roots.

I leaned back from the bed and wiped my forehead before droplets could run down my nose. She rolled on her back. The bed springs sounded like a rusted car driving over bumps in a road.

I rubbed her temples until she breathed deeply. I stopped. The time was late. Everyone in the mission, except me, was probably asleep. The frogs and crickets, of course, were still awake.

A strong wind appeared. It rattled the leaves in the trees and the bushes, warning of an approaching storm. I checked the fire where I cooked. The wind had blown away the ashes, leaving red coals exposed. I rolled rocks on them with my feet to prevent sparking embers from flying away and igniting my wood pile.

I wandered the grounds, walking aimlessly, fighting the feelings that wanted to jump out of me—feelings I feared, feelings that seemed to have been building my entire life, first with Father and now with Mother Stevens. I released the knots in my bound fists. I shook them at my sides, easing the tingling in my fingers.

The smell of rain entered me. I stood as erect as my back would allow. My feet knew they were on the road to Monrovia, but it was too black for my eyes to see it. Then, ahead of me, lightning flashed. The road, for an instant, became a tunnel of shadows and light. I waited for the thunder—God's voice, I used to believe. It came rolling in, deep and loud, booming all around me, shaking the air as if God gripped it with his hands. When I was a child, I had hidden under Zena's bed with her. Now I remained in the open. If God was angry with me, then he might also want to punish me.

My feet found the trail that lead to the river. I ran. More lightening, casting my flying limbs among the shadows of the trees. A frightening sight as they seemed to reach to grab me. God spoke again. His wrath had killed many before. Why not me?

The rain hit me without warning, powered by a blast of enraged wind. I tripped and fell, tumbling into a bush. In an instant, I was soaked. The downpour created its own voice, hurling itself against the trees, creating sounds in the leaves that were warning me to run. More lightening. More of God's irate voice.

I scrambled deeper into the bushes. Thorns pricked and cut me, but I was safe from God. I curled into a ball, put my hands over my face, and I prayed, "Jesus, help me. Please, please help me." My words were cries, barely spoken, barely heard in my own ears. Screaming, I said, "Jesus, hear my voice; it's Jabonkah."

He knew me by name. It was supposed to be written down in some book in Heaven. He could check it and see my name meant "God remembers." Why would he need to search for it in his book, I reasoned? More violence, more wind, more rain, more lightening.

My body shook uncontrollably. I could barely keep my palms pressed together and hold them close to my lips. I began to sing, thinking of Paul and Silus when they were in prison, when they sang hymns, and their chains fell off. "Jesus loves the little children." That was all that I could sing. I repeated it over and over and over, "Jesus loves the little children."

I remained in the bushes, sharp points scratching me as the wind yanked the bush's limbs, trying to shake me out from hiding. I remembered Elijah who had hid in a cave like I hid in the bush. The impulse to leave the protection and security of my prickly nest was slight at first, but then the more I pictured Elijah on his knees outside the cave, where he had been hiding in fear of death, the greater my urge became to come out, even as the storm continued to rage.

After several uncertain tries, I crawled out on my knees and hands. The trail was muddy and slippery. The smell of the ocean was strong. I gathered courage, shaking like a lone leaf on a storm-stripped branch. Exposed, in the open, I lifted to my knees. I prayed, "Lord Jesus, please take me to Heaven to be with you." God's thunder spoke, but I didn't return to hiding. "Or save me from this place, these boys, and Mother Stevens."

I stood. The thunder and lightning continued. I felt a sense of acceptance of what might come. I held out my arms and pulled back my face to allow the rain to remove the clinging mud and sticking leaves from me. Lowering my arms, I scrubbed away any remaining dirt. I walked back to the mission, heading toward the storage room, finding it warm and dry.

I lay down on the rough canvas of many empty rice sacks. Another storm followed the one that was leaving. There would be no fire in the morning to cook breakfast. The boys would go hungry. Let them, I thought. I have been hungry for sixteen rice fields.

# 38
# Over the Ocean

While ironing Mother Stevens's sheets, I noticed the scratches on my arm, which were now healed and only slightly visible, that I had received several weeks ago while thinking I was Elijah hiding in his cave. That same night, I had stepped on a thorn. Mother Stevens had dug it out of my right foot after it had turned red with infection, swelling, hurting, making me hobble, noticeable then to Mother Stevens.

God and I seemed to have come to a point in our relationship where we both had said what we needed to say, laying down our deepest feelings at the feet of the other. And now we waited, a period of drought, no rain, no lightening, no thunder—God's voice was silent.

I lifted the iron, hissing steam came from the bottom. I sat it on the metal resting plate. When I had first tried to iron, I had burned several holes in Mother Stevens's linens. Whippings did seem to help me concentrate.

God had made his decision. He didn't want me in Heaven. Perhaps, he had the same opinion of me as everyone else, worthless—well...except for Zena and Grandma Crowcoco and Grandpa and Miss Johnson and Mrs.

Abkey and Miss Palmer and Mother Holmes.

I leaned on the windowsill of the laundry room. The boys played football, creating a cloud of reddish dust as they all bunched up and fought for the ball. They would be hungry soon. I needed to iron faster. I was out of time and still had one sheet left.

The iron hissed again as I lifted it. I had favorites among the boys. I was sister to many, rubbing sore, aching legs. I suspected some of the legs were fine, and those boys wanted me to rub their legs because they were lonely.

I was always tired, drained to the point of not wanting to eat, feeling more aching bones in my body each new day. My back hurt all the time. I had developed a slight limp. Some of the boys made fun of me, mimicking me, while other boys helped, when they could, after school and before evening chapel.

Lifting the end of the white apron Mother Stevens insisted I wear, I wiped down my temples and forehead.

Mother yelled, "Jeanette."

Her voice was similar to God's thunder. Both made me tremble. I ran to the other window. Mother Stevens stood in the doorway with her hands on her hips.

"Jeanette!"

It was her whipping voice.

As I ran to leave, I smelled the iron scorching Mother Stevens's sheet. I caught it just in time, before it had made a mark. Outside, I knew I needed to start the fire, but she didn't know that. I had emptied her pot and swept her floor. My steps slowed as I got closer.

When she saw me coming from across the yard, she went inside. I had already boiled the well water, cooled it, and poured it into her clean plastic bottles. She had snacks, bananas, mangos, and butter pears.

What did I forget this time? Maybe it was a spider she needed me to kill or a snake—maybe I had left the screen window open to her room and a snake had slipped in. Whatever it was, it was a beating for sure.

"Where are you? What is taking you so long?" she yelled from the living room.

"I'm here, ma'am." Inside, I took slower steps. She sat at her desk, maybe writing a letter before she whipped me.

"Come here." The corners of her eyes were *not* pulled tight and her lips were *not* pressed together so that her chin stuck out.

"I'm here now, ma'am," I said. My knees felt loose, like I was entering the outhouse with the snakes.

Her face broke into a smile. I leaned forward, pulled toward her by some force. "How would you like to go to America? To get an education!" I jumped, startled by her obvious excitement and amazed by her words—go to America!

Her smile flipped over into a frown. "I said, 'How would you like to go to America?' not pee on my floor!" Her frown remained. She turned back to her desk and began to write on her yellow stationary with the brown swirling edges. "Clean that up."

"Yes, ma'am." I ran to the bathroom and grabbed the towel she used to step on when she got out of her bath. I stuck an edge of it under the faucet and made it wet.

"That Randy."

Her voice sounded disgusted. She talked louder as I was in the bathroom wiping myself. "That boy stole his own tuition money. I can hardly believe it." I returned to the living room. She was shaking her head. I got on my knees to wipe up, trembling in disbelief, worried that Mother Stevens would change her mind at any second.

"He and I were at his school. I had his tuition money in an envelope, lying on the desk, while we waited for the secretary to fetch a new receipt book from the supply closet. I went to the bathroom. I came back just minutes later and Randy was gone." She slammed the palms of her hands down on her desk. I cringed. "He took the money!"

I checked to see if I'd peed again. Mother Stevens was *so* upset.

"All this time." She looked over her shoulder at me. "He blamed you. When he was probably the one stealing…all these years."

I nodded.

She began to write again. "I'm writing my home church in Oakland. That's in California. And I am going to find you a sponsor. I've saved five hundred dollars that I was going to use to send Randy, but now…I'm sending you."

I ran, holding myself, fearing I would pee on Mother Stevens's floor again, causing her to change her mind and not send me over the ocean. When I got outside, I stopped.

Some boys worked at making a fire under the big black pot. White smoke rose but no flames. I wanted to turn around and go back and ask

Mother Stevens if it were true—I was going over the ocean, free of this place, free of these boys, free of her voice and whip.

I thought of Lot's wife, when she and Lot fled the destruction of Gomorrah. Would I turn to stone, like her, if I looked back? I paused and pondered, thinking I knew why she had looked back. I had never understood it before. It seemed so simple that she should just listen to her husband.

She had family, brothers, sisters, nieces and nephews, perhaps even parents, her mother, like my Zena. Mother Stevens said she was writing a letter to find me a…sponsor, whatever that was. She was driving me away from the mission, Liberia, Africa, my home, Zena. It was what I had prayed for. God had answered my prayer so why look back? Her word had always been good. Why doubt her?

I started walking again. I didn't look back. I picked up a stick, raised it in the air, and drove the boys as if they were blackbirds eating rice in the field. I laughed at their fright. They said words Mother Stevens should never hear from them.

I lit a fire. The smell of burning wood reminded me of Zena, my dear Zena whom I had wanted to be like and never be separated from. I walked to the well for water and felt the rolling of tears on my face, tears not from leaving Zena but from knowing I could. I got the rice for dinner. And, only then, did I look back at Mother Stevens's house.

# 39
# The Letter

Mother Stevens wrote to her Baptist Church in Oakland, California, and asked them to sponsor me. Mother may have asked more than one person to provide me housing, but the only person I was aware of was Miss Viola Moore.

Mother Stevens asked me to write Mother Moore a letter. I had never written a letter before. It went something like this.

*My name is Jeanette Stevens. How would you like a daughter? I want to come to America to live with you.*

The day after the blue truck had driven away with my letter to Mother Moore, the blue truck returned late in the day with the mail from Monrovia, which I had never cared about before. All my chores were done, cleaning up from supper and washing bowl after bowl after bowl, so I ran to Mother Stevens's house. The man in the blue truck had taken a handful of things to her. I thought some of the items he carried might have been a letter from Mother Moore. On his way back to his truck, the driver smiled at me.

Mother Stevens had finished her supper: her special rice without the weevils, leftover fried chicken, potato greens, sliced tomatoes, and a bowl of cut fruit (mangos, butter pears, sweet oranges, and banana, all of which I sprinkled with shreds of toasted coconut). I walked to her bedroom. The door was open. I tiptoed in. She rested on her bed, taking a nap. Her toes pointed up. Her breathing was shallow. She was not asleep, but her eyes were closed.

I waited by her bed.

Moments passed until Mother Stevens said, "Yes, Jeanette, what is it? Can't you see I'm resting?"

I had never disturbed her in this way, but my curiosity was so great that I had to ask about the mail. "Forgive me, ma'am, but I was…" Suddenly I wondered if I upset her she would change her mind about sending me to America.

"Yes, Jeanette." Her voice was soft. She was not angry.

"Did the man in the blue truck bring a letter from Mother Moore?"

Her stomach bounced up and down as she laughed. "Silly, silly, girl. It will take weeks to hear from Viola."

I didn't feel silly. I didn't know how letters worked. But, thinking about the map of the world and how Oakland was on the other side of the Earth, I felt stupid, like when the boys teased me about those things they knew and I didn't.

She stopped laughing and said, "We have many things to work out, but we shall get you to America." She rolled on her right side, facing away from me. "Go now. You smell like smoke."

I sensed a new relationship developing between Mother Stevens and me. She was driving me away. Maybe she knew my body was broken. Maybe she knew my spirit was broken. Was she the answer to my prayers? Maybe God had spoken with her again. I wondered who would take my place. Certainly not Randy. He was lazy.

After Mother Stevens had decided to send me to America to get an education, Randy didn't come home from school as she wanted. He may have slept in the white van or stayed with friends. I was thankful that she never spoke again of my marriage to Randy. He needed a woman he could rule. God knew that no man would rule over me. Had God really spoken to Mother Stevens about my marriage to Randy? I wished God would remind her of the times she had beaten me when it was Randy who had lied and stolen things. I remembered.

Every day, I kept watch for the blue truck. To my dismay, its arrival was unpredictable. He came early morning while I was serving the boys their oats, which forced me to wait and wonder if I had a return letter from Mother Moore. Or the truck arrived in a cloud of red dust with the driver honking his horn, teasing me, knowing I was desperate for a letter from America. Naturally, I reminded him each day I was waiting for a letter, in case he had forgotten. I also told him the letter would be addressed to me.

Once, his breath stank of palm wine, and he smiled at me for no reason. He was missing one of his front teeth. He stared at me in a way that embarrassed me about being a woman. And, on this same day, he said that he had the letter I had been waiting for and told me I may not have it unless I got in the truck with him. I knew he was lying. The boys had taught me how to tell. They acted nice if they wanted something. Besides, who would believe a drunken man?

Weeks later, I finally received a return letter from Mother Moore. It read:

*Dearest Jeanette,*

*Yes, I would love to have you come and stay with me and be my daughter. I am sixty years old and have no children. I have always wanted a daughter, but I never married. God has blessed my life with other work and for that I am grateful. Yes, there were times I had prayed for a family, but God in His wisdom waited until now to answer my prayers.*

*I have a large, two-story, four-bedroom home which is near the high school, near the market, and just five blocks away from our wonderful church. We bought new hymnals last month, as our other ones were so old the covers were falling off and pages were missing. Of course, I have memorized most of the hymns we sing; nevertheless, we were concerned about our visitors and the youth having proper hymnals.*

*Please write me again, Jeanette, and tell me more about your family and your life in Africa.*

*In Our Savior's Name,*

*Viola Moore*

That night, after I had rubbed Mother Stevens to sleep, I went to the storage hut; I took a candle, matches, writing paper, and the pencil that had the best eraser. I made many mistakes. That had been the first letter I had ever received, the only thing that was completely mine. Mother Stevens had bought me new dresses, but I hated wearing them. I didn't claim them as mine. I preferred to dress like the boys, who wore loose-fitting T-shirts and ragged shorts.

The usual woody smell of the bush was gone. A strong wind carried ocean brine so thick I imagined that if I were to lick my lips, I would taste salt, but I knew that it would have been my own sweat.

After I had entered the hut, I lit the candle. I dragged four rice sacks to the middle of the room, using one hand, holding the glowing candle in my right hand. I stuck the candle in between two sacks, twisting it in deep so that it would not fall over. Now with both hands, careful of my back, I stacked another pair of sacks in front of the flickering light. This is how I usually constructed my alter. I would rest my elbows on the scratchy surface and put my palms together and pray, sometimes until I fell asleep.

This time, I pounded the top sack flat with my fists, then smoothed it with my palms. I placed sheets of lined school paper on my sack-desk. I sat. The paper was dark. The flame was too low for me to see to write. I quickly pulled two more sacks together and built up the crack that held the candle.

I squatted. The lines appeared. I knelt and centered the paper. I was ready to begin. I laid Mother Moore's letter, which was on light blue paper and had AIR MAIL printed on it with a drawing of an airplane, next to my empty sheet. Mother Stevens had told me that Mother Moore's type of paper was called parchment, thin like the pages of a Bible. I reread Mother Moore's letter at least six times, especially the part where she thought that I, Jabonkah Sackey, might be an answer to her prayers for a daughter.

I experienced new feelings. I had heard for so long that I would never amount to anything, which only made me more determined to amount to something, but I had no idea how to do this other than praying. It was hard to believe that I could be the answer to someone's prayers. I had prayed for so long to receive God's mercy that I came to believe he didn't remember me. Did he love me this much to finally respond to my pleas to be rescued? Why had he taken so long? I tried not to be angry for his delay, but that would take time to forgive.

I laid my body over the pages and put my nose next to the smoking wax. I looked at the rigid flame, burning in a plume of yellow, blue, white, and red, creating dim light for the room, yet it burned bright in my eyes.

Tears formed. I closed my eyelids before they leaked. I breathed deeply. I smelled the grains and meal. I smiled with thoughts of Zena and the rice fields, where I drove away the birds that were merely hungry. Perhaps God drove people who were hungry for something other than food to a place where they would be satisfied.

A chill came over me, a tingle that made the hairs on my body stand on end. My eyes opened, and I found the sight of the candle reassuring. I sat straight. The tingling went away. I had crumpled my pages and torn the seam of Mother Moore's letter.

I picked up the drooping pages and held them to my chest where my heart raced as if I had been running. I looked to the ceiling where there seemed to be more than crossing boards. I sensed God was looking down on me with the kindness of a father I had never known.

Another outbreak of chills consumed me. "Thank you, Father," I said with a muttering, exhaled breath. I closed my eyes and listened for the sound of God's voice, fully expecting an answer. I waited and waited and waited, feeling a kernel of rice under my left knee, as I rocked back and forth. Time was not recognizable. My mind raced with the possibility that God actually knew me. He really cared. My spirit lifted, shedding years of misery and doubt. I felt free and happy like no other time. Not even with Zena had I known such joy.

I stood and jumped up in the air, bouncing repeatedly, ignoring the pain in my back. I wanted to scream, but waking two hundred boys and Mother could not happen. I stopped. Stood straight. Pulled my head back. Lifting my arms, stretching my fingers apart, standing up on my toes, I expected God to lift me up to him and hold me like a loving father. I felt him. Here. Now.

The tingling needles in my hands became unbearable. I lowered them along with my body to the coolness of the concrete floor. Mother Moore's letter lay next to me, upside-down. I grabbed it then leaped to the light to reread it. Yes, it was true—she wanted a daughter. I lay down, holding the letter in my arms as if it were a newly born child.

# 40
# Letters That Spoke the Truth

Letters That Spoke the Truth

I had fallen asleep before I could write to Mother Moore. I was already in the storage hut, but I knew there would be no time to pray if I was to feed two hundred hungry boys. I hid her letter and my paper and pencil under a sack of rolled oats.

While I went through my routine, as I had done every day except when school was out and the children were gone, I thought of Mother Moore. She wanted to know about my life in Africa. I didn't know where to start; besides, I lived in Bomi Hills, not Africa.

I wanted to tell her all about Zena, but thinking about Zena made me forget about Mother Moore and the letter I needed to write. Most every memory I had included Zena. My wonderful Zena. From first learning I would go over the ocean, I considered that I might never see her again or hear her say, "Too many words, Jabonkah. Too many words."

My insides smiled.

Yes, I had too many words, but which ones should I use in a letter to

Mother Moore? I began to worry about leaving Zena. "Sister, I'm waiting." It was a boy who wanted his bowl filled with oats. I plopped him some gooey paste. The next boy held his skinny arms out. I realized that I no longer wanted to be a bush woman. I wanted to be a different woman. One no one else ruled. I didn't know what would happen to me across the ocean. But now I had a new mother waiting for me in America. One who wanted me and seemed to want to love me. This excited but scared me. Happy to be wanted, but afraid I was being given away for a second time.

I decided that any life that didn't include this mission and these needy boys was better. This was Mother Stevens's purpose for living, not mine.

So in my first letter to Mother Moore, I told her how Mother Stevens had been so loving and generous and how grateful I was for all she had done for me. Partly this was true, and knowing that Mother Stevens would read what I had written, I decided not to write how I really felt.

It was not until my third letter to Mother Moore that Mother Stevens allowed me to send my letters directly, without her first reading them. But after the very first letter I sent, I tore up the ones that Mother Stevens had approved. I wrote new ones that spoke the truth. This was deceitful, and I felt guilty, but for the first time in eight years someone cared about me and wanted to know all about me.

I told Mother Moore how I had suffered and how I prayed God would take me to Heaven or answer my prayers to leave the mission, but I had not known where to ask God to send me. I just wanted to be free from here, and—I wanted to amount to something. I knew I could not fit all of this on one page.

I wrote many letters, even before I received responses from Mother Moore. I had so much to tell her, and she wanted to learn more about me and my life. I wrote and wrote and wrote the same words that God had heard for the past four years.

I saved all of my allowance to use for postage. I was nice to the man in the blue truck. If I paid him money, he was glad to take my letters and buy stamps for me.

I tried to smile all the time. I became alert to do all the boys needed and especially whatever Mother Stevens asked. I was going to America to answer Mother Moore's prayer, to receive a new mother, and to get an education.

One afternoon, Mother Stevens yelled my name in her sharp-as-usual voice. I stood over a hot kettle, in the direct afternoon sun, boiling cassava leaves. The boys were in class. I froze and assumed the worst had happened—I could not go to America.

My steps always felt heavy when I walked to her house, even when she was not calling out for me. I feared I would lose my freedom before I possessed it. My feet seemed weighted as if stuck in my biggest black pots.

Mother Stevens stood next to her desk, holding a letter. She had unbuttoned the top of her white blouse. Beads of perspiration covered her upper lip, which seemed to annoy her, because she kept wiping it with a white handkerchief that she kept wadded in her hand.

The paper she held was typed and had a colorful seal at the top. It was an official government document. Mother Stevens seemed concerned, not angry.

"Yes, ma'am?"

She lowered the letter to her waist and looked at me as if she needed something. "Jeanette, we must have your parents' signatures."

John Henry, my father? My fears grew and my hopes shriveled. "Why?"

Lifting the letter in her hand, she pressed her thumb against the bottom, causing the paper to stiffen into a curve. She used it to fan her face.

"I don't want you to go on a student visa. They might not renew it, and you'd have to come back. I want you to go as an immigrant and become a citizen." She shook her head as she waved the paper. "The problem is, you are not eighteen…and I never legally adopted you. That's why you need your mother and father's signatures."

"What if he is dead?"

She stopped cooling herself and turned. "Why would you say that?"

Her eyes were sharp and seemed to search me for the answer. I felt she had discovered the place where I had buried the hatred for my father. I shrugged. I rubbed the top of my right foot with my left. If I had wanted to kill him, surely others in his *kingdom* might have felt the same way.

Mother Stevens's face changed again. Her eyes opened and the lines in her forehead grew deeper. She leaned her head back and fanned. "Jeanette, your father did what was best for you." She paused, perhaps sensing my disagreement. "You'll understand when you're older," she said, with a dismissive tone.

I wondered how old Grandma Crowcoco was. I might have to be as old and wrinkled as her to find forgiveness for Father. I remembered the color of Zena's blood as it ran down her back and the black emptiness in her eyes.

It was true. I still hated my father. It enraged me to think that I needed *his* permission to go to America. And for Mother Stevens to tell me that he had done what was best for me, as if the past four years had never existed. It seemed like yesterday that I had wanted my father dead. I still did. I could imagine no other justice for him. I know God wanted me to forgive him. But this was not possible. Not now and maybe not forever.

*He's the devil,* I wanted to shout to Mother Stevens.

She sat at her desk. I examined my feet, not wanting to look at her. The legs of her chair made sharp complaints as she scooted closer to her desk. She said, "Dead or alive, we must know, and he must sign; and if he is dead, your mother can sign."

My violent thoughts switched to hope. The heaviness of existence reversed and peacefulness returned. "But…Zena can't write," I said. Mother looked up from her papers and stared at the picture of Jesus that hung on the wall, the one where he knelt praying against a boulder, looking up to Heaven.

"Jeanette, if it is God's will for you to go to America, then he shall open all the doors."

"Mother, how many more doors are there?"

"Yes, you must know." She turned her to face me. "I didn't want to worry you…there are three doors." She wiped her lip dry. "First of all, you have no sponsor. Certain members of the church board are fearful you will become pregnant or you will be unable to resist the drugs that the youth are experimenting with. Then there is your…well, the results of your physical exam came back and you have been exposed to tuberculosis."

Mother paused.

I said, "What does 'exposed to tuberculosis' mean?"

"You carry the tuberculosis virus…which could infect others if it became active."

I breathed in deeply and exhaled. "I don't feel anything."

Mother's lips thinned as she smiled. "You wouldn't, child." Her smile flew away. Her eyebrows drew together. "I could still send you as a student, since your education is lacking, but that I should be able to work out. They might accept you on a probationary basis. But this is a last resort. Then again, that would give us time. Time to convince the dissenting members of the board that you're a sweet girl and have no such…" Mother Stevens stopped. She seemed uncomfortable. "…such thoughts of boys." Mother went back to her writing.

I stepped into the sunshine and entered a hoard of mosquitoes that were out early, before the cooler evening. I was anxious about the three doors that needed to open for me to go to America: the tuberculosis that lived in me, finding a sponsor, and getting Father to sign, if he was still alive. I wondered how I would get Father to come to talk to Mother Stevens. I walked into the bush, squatted, and thought about writing a letter to Father, but if he were dead—Randy. This was the first time I needed something from him, and I hoped it would be the last.

Yes, I decided, I must ask Randy to get my father. I would pay him. He would do anything for money.

# 41

# Butterflies

I had to give Randy five dollars and forty-five cents, the last of my money. He made me swear on a Bible that this was all the money I had. After I lifted my hand from my New Testament, I said, "So hurry and get my father." Randy seemed to ignore me as he unwadded the dollar bills I had given him. He flattened them one at a time against the smooth bark of a Cyprus tree, which grew near the river, where we met in secret. Mother would suspect something if she saw us together and not arguing. He held the bills at the ends and moved them back and forth, like I had with a cloth across Father's shoes to shine them.

"Hold your horses there, partner." Randy was a big fan of the western movies he saw in Monrovia. "Just what am I supposed to say to your father?" He stuffed each bill into a ripped and faded wallet, which had holes and looked as if a dog had buried it and Randy had dug it up years later.

I sat on my heels, looking up at his tallness, catching the coins that kept falling from the rip in the bottom of his wallet. I handed them back to him. Finally, he stuck his finger through the hole and wiggled it. He stuffed the coins in the sides of his faded-red tennis shoes. I assumed he had holes in the pockets of his tattered green shorts, or he would have put them there. He must have had money to buy new clothes, but he spent his money on other things, things I didn't know or care to know about. He would have bought a cowboy hat if they had sold them in Monrovia.

"Well? What do I tell him?" He had finished putting the coins in his shoe. He turned his backside to me and put his wallet into his ripped back pocket. The wallet was larger than the hole in his pocket. He sat on his heels a few feet away, facing me. He smelled like a boy, sour and salty.

I also wondered what would make Father want to come to the mission to give me permission to go to America. I looked into Randy's big eyes, which were full of red lines. We stared at each other, neither looking away. Then he shoved me backward. I struggled to break my fall, arms flying behind me, preventing my head from landing in the thorns.

He began to laugh. "I would never have married you. You're just a *bush* woman."

Anger rushed in me. I sprang up.

Randy stood and stared down at me. His fists were closed, like mine. I had to go to America. Father had to come. I needed Randy to get him.

"Please, Randy. I'm sorry Mother Stevens changed her mind. I know you must be sad, but this is my chance to get away from here."

I reached for his hands.

He slapped them away. "I'm not getting your father. You did this to me. Now my life is destroyed, because of you!" He had tears welling in his eyes. "Besides, you're an idiot, stupid as a frog, and the ugliest girl I've ever seen." He turned his face to wipe his eyes.

"No, Randy, it's all because you're a thief! It's *your* fault Mother Stevens is sending me and not you!" Rage quickly consumed me. I screamed at him. "I got the beatings you should have gotten!" I stepped closer to him. "And I'm not a stupid bush woman! And I would run away before I ever married you!"

A mean expression with angry eyes and pressed lips appeared on his face, then he said, "You're not fit to marry, you've been—"

He stopped.

He knew? Or he assumed I had been to the Society?

Grief sprouted in me, growing from my stomach, spreading through my body until a fierce sadness reached my toes and fingers. My chest drew tight. My throat collapsed, feeling like an elephant was stepping on it, preventing me from taking my next breath.

I turned and ran toward the trail, where thick bushes tried to pinch it closed and vines grabbed me at as if trying to stop me. I didn't look back but heard Randy yelling. "Jeanette. Stop. Wait up." His voice drew further away. I knew he was running after me but slower, because he was so much bigger and the brush thicker for him.

The trail split. I took the old one that was all but closed off that led toward the waterfall. Sticky spider webs clung to my face. The more I ran, the more Randy's voice faded. He was giving up. The path was too tight for him. I had escaped. I slowed, dropped to my hands and knees, and crawled, weeping, not able to wipe my tears with my muddy hands. I wanted to lie down, but I kept going, resisting the urge to stop and have the bush grow over me, let it absorb me into the decayed leaves as it does with all other dead things. I crawled and crawled and crawled until the rushing water of the falls was all I could hear.

I squirmed on my stomach, clearing the bush, and rested on the muddy bank. Through a gap in the heavy cloud of trees, the sharp sun burned the back of my neck and legs. The mist from the falling water rose and swirled high and fell at the same time. The mist seemed eager to fall to the rocks below. Something in me wanted to join the water and become part of the falling mist. A wasp buzzed, hovered near my face, then landed next to me. It folded its black and yellow wings. Its spiny legs floated on top, while my heart pounded a hole in the mud.

"Do you want her? She will never amount to anything." I heard my father's voice in my mind. I saw now what I hadn't seen then, how Mother Stevens had first looked at me, like a banana she was going to buy.

I was not a bush woman. I was not a lady like Miss Palmer in the bank. I was not going to America to get an education because Father would never come.

Guilt crept out from somewhere, exposing what I had not yet decided. It was a sin. Unforgiveable. But the pain would be gone. Over with.

"Jeanette."

It was Randy. I had not heard him from the roar of the falls. He lifted me and swayed as he walked in ankle deep mud. He carried me and held me, and I broke into more tears than an entire day of rain. I slung my arms around his neck, feeling the heat of his body and my pounding heart against his. He still smelled like a boy, but I didn't care.

"Education, Jeanette. Your father never wanted you to be a stupid bush woman. He wanted you to get an education."

I shook my head. "He won't come."

"He'll come and sign those papers you need."

I shook my head more, longing for Randy to say it again in his confident voice. "He hates me."

"You were probably a thorn up his ass."

"He beat us."

"You deserved it. Look at you now: hardheaded and damn near illiterate. He could have given you away to another tribe or to men who sell stupid bush girls like you. Are you really this stupid? He gave you to Mother Stevens, so maybe you'd learn something."

I squirmed and pushed away from him. "Let me down." He released me fast, and I fell to the ground, landing on my butt, my tailbone sending burning pain across my bottom and up my back.

"You bastard!" I stood, rubbing my bottom, curling my back. "You hurt me."

"You're an ugly mess. You're muddy from head to toe. And look at me." He held his arms open and to the side. "Now I'm a mess too." He had a spot of mud on the end of his nose.

I began to laugh, hard and loud.

"What?" He smiled with a grin that replaced the aching in my tailbone with hundreds of butterflies tickling my stomach. I touched my nose. He looked cross-eyed at his. The butterflies wanted to break free.

# 42
# Indigestion

This day Randy was leaving to get Father. I had prepared one of Mother Stevens's special containers, filling it full of cooked rice and dried fish. It would take a lot of food to keep Randy motivated to walk all the way to Bomi Hills. I was not sure of the distance, but he would need at least three meals to get there. Zena would see that he had food for his walk back.

Randy was ready to leave, but he complained that he was already hungry. I had anticipated this and had saved him oats from breakfast. We sat on a log outside the mission. I didn't want Mother Stevens to see I was using one of her special containers for Randy. Of course, she would not have trusted Randy with her container, and neither did I, so I told him that she would beat him if he didn't bring it back. He said she would not. He was right, so I promised to give him my next two allowances if he returned with it. Otherwise, she would beat *me*.

Randy waited patiently while I sliced a ripe butter pear on top of his oats, the way he liked it. His faded-red T-shirt was already soaked with sweat. Before he left, I would get him one of Mother Stevens's special water bottles to take with him. This was the dry season, and the streams were extra muddy.

"Do you know what you are going to say?" I said.

He spoke with his mouth full, showing me the white of the oats and the green of the butter pear. "I told you already," he said. "Mother Stevens wants to send you to America to get an education." He took a scoop of food so large I expected his jaw to unhinge to make room in his mouth. "And she needs his signature on some form."

"But will he come? I'm afraid he won't." I twisted the loose end of a dangling dreadlock and tugged at it until it sprang free of its weave. "It is a very long walk, and he does not care about me and probably wishes I was dead."

Randy didn't break his rhythm, spoon to bowl to mouth to bowl to mouth, seeming not to chew. He garbled his words. "Well, so what if he doesn't come." Randy burped. "The waterfall is still there." He glanced at me, away from his precious food.

I stopped twisting my hair and stared at him. I hated him. "What do you mean by that?"

He looked into his food and scraped the edges of the bowl to get the last of the oats and pear. "Nothing. He will come if I have to force him with his life." He met my eyes. "You deserve this fate, not me."

The butterflies I had felt when Randy had pulled me from the mud returned, but I decided it was probably indigestion.

# 43
# The Tall Man and Short Woman

Randy left as soon as he had finished eating. I made certain. I pulled on him, forced him to stand, then pushed him from behind, until he finally became angry and started to swat at me. He told me he was leaving only because it was still a cool part of the day not because I was forcing him.

He left. That was Friday.

On Saturday mornings after breakfast, I helped the boys clean their dormitory, which meant I did most of the work. The floor was one long stretch of concrete and was covered with dirt, dusty with bugs, both dead and alive, mostly roaches and crickets. Once in a while, I found small snakes hiding under dirty clothes and scattered blankets. They ate the roaches and crickets.

If it were not for Mother Stevens's insistence and my efforts, the lazy boys would never shake out their bedding or drape it over the sills of the open windows. On their raised cots, they lived happily above the filth and crawling things. It was hot sweaty work, but I didn't mind.

Sunday mornings were the busiest days, cooking and getting the boys ready for church. Usually, I had very little time for myself, and today, the day I would keep watch on the road for the tall man and short woman, I was late.

I had bathed and squeezed lime juice not only under my arms but also on my face and neck. I slipped into my best dress—not my Christmas dress as I had outgrown that one, mostly in the chest. My breasts had become big like the vegetables that grew large in my garden.

Mother Stevens led the singing at the front of the sanctuary, and boys stood from their seats. The church was filled with song. I was too distracted to care what they sang. The chapel was stifling hot. I hid behind the tallest group, hoping that she would not notice I was late for worship. She didn't put up with such disrespect. This was the Lord's time. Most likely, she had already discovered my absence.

I recognized the hymn. I sang the chorus but had to wait to know which verse was next. I joined the verse and sang happily to the end, smiling and raising my hands to God, praising him for his creation and his love and for his bringing Father and Zena here today—I hoped—while I kept looking behind me out the door and down the road for the tall man and short woman.

Worship had ended, but the music continued to play in my heart. The peace and contentment in the hope Father was on his way also sustained me. I had cooked with both of my largest kettles to make enough rice and cassava greens for Sunday's abundance dinner. Mother Stevens insisted that the boys be well fed on Sundays, full of the Lord and full of rice.

After everyone had eaten, the boys played football, tag, or just ran crazy, creating lots of dust and horrible noises. I grew more anxious with the lengthening of every shadow. My heart raced, pounding in my ears with a ringing that caused me to sit next to the swing in the shade. From there, I watched for the tall man and short woman or Randy, who might have crushing news.

I snapped a small twig, then gently broke it along the grain, creating a splinter. I poked at the crevices in between my teeth, cleaning them. After I was done, I started over, but this time I pushed harder, enjoying the pain and the earthy taste of blood. I tried not to think about what I would do if Father refused to come. My hopes had grown into a heavy bunch of fruit that strained against the branches of my faith.

"Mmmmmm." I jammed a back molar, where my gum had already

become swollen from my last cleaning.

The growing shadows told me, along with the boys' quietness, that supper must be started soon. Still, I sat on my heels. I rocked up on the balls of my feet then let myself back down. I prayed and prayed and prayed, my eyes never leaving the road. I drove away the birds of doubt with the biggest stick my silent prayers could manage. I breathed deeply, like women do in childbirth.

The wind blew the white cotton clouds, which gave and took away the light, creating shadows that seemed to move on the tree-lined road. I had to determine which shadows were free to roam, unlike the shadows of the trees that were slaves to the ground.

Suddenly, I saw free-moving shadows. The figures were easy to see— the tall man and short woman. I wondered if I had dozed, because they were so close.

It had to be Father in his white shirt and dark slacks with two other men behind him. Two tribesmen who held the ends of two long poles that dangled a bulging canvas, filled, no doubt, with gifts of food. Bush people had no other treasures.

Zena. It was Zena to the side of them, my friend and the best mother any child could have had. Before I realized it, I was running as fast as my legs would move without toppling onto my face. Through a blur, I saw the burdens on Zena's back, head, and in her arms. She seemed more like a pack animal who carried almost as much as the men did together.

Before I flung myself into her, like when I was a needy child of eight rice fields, Zena dropped her loads and stretched out her arms. We were the same height. Her smile was wide. So was mine. The holes in her cheeks reminded me of my own, but she seemed much older.

She remembered how I had lain my head on her left shoulder and hugged under her arms. We wailed in unison, a chorus that was both mournful and rejoicing. We stood as one shadow for some time until we were both wet with the other's sweat and tears.

We finally broke apart, but I held her cheeks and kissed and kissed and kissed her, saying over and over, "Zena, I missed you." Finally her face was wet with kisses. She was laughing so hard, she pushed me away, it seemed, to grab back her breath.

I picked up the gauze-covered slab of dried pork. "Come meet Mother Stevens." Zena wore a blank face of confusion. I tried to speak Gola, but I only remembered the words "rice" and "monkey bridge," the latter renewed her wrinkled smile. "Come," I said and motioned with my head.

The boys had gathered around Father and Mother Stevens, but when Zena and I approached the others, they opened a path for us to enter the circle. There he stood—John Henry—maybe the devil or just a man; it didn't change what he had done. He didn't look at me.

"Jeanette, come," Mother Stevens said, more a command than a request.

I set the salted pork on the porch of Mother Stevens's house, then helped Zena with the pot of rice and greens. The village men had brought two large quarters of aged cow meat, the blues and greens of age covered it. They lay the quarters at Mother's feet, like an offering, but I knew that it was a custom that showed respect. I was certain that Father had never sought forgiveness from anyone.

"What shall we do with all of this food?" Mother Stevens said, giving me a rare smile. Father seemed mild, gentle, almost bashful, contrary to my memories of him, except for the times he had been with the white men at the mining company.

I knew the boys were hungry, and I was late starting their supper. "I'll give it to the boys, if that's okay, ma'am."

"Yes, feed the children." Mother Stevens didn't seem interested in meeting Zena. She smoothed her already neat hair, then took Father and the two village men on a tour of the mission. Zena and I carried all of the food to the cooking area, while the boys danced around us, asking when we would eat.

# 44
# Mother Stevens Ruled

Because of the additional food, there were extra dishes to clean, bones to scatter to the stray dogs, and pots to scrape, but with Zena's help, we finished about the same time I normally did, which was surprising. We kept staring at each other and smiling, grinning, and hugging while we prepared the meal and cleaned up afterward.

All this time, Zena tried to tell me something in her Gola language. We laughed, and we tried to figure out what she wanted to say that hugs and kisses could not communicate. I kept shrugging. She spoke louder, as if that would help me understand her language, one I had not heard or spoken for four years.

Finally, after we were finished with the dishes, she grabbed my left hand in her rougher and stronger hand, looked different directions, then dragged me to the edge of the mission and stopped where the wild roses grew. She released my hand and cupped hers around, but not touching, the most beautiful flower on a rose bush. She drew her hands away from the flower, keeping them cupped, saying something in Gola that included my name, then placed her hands on either side of my face.

I took her wrists and backed them gently to her face and said, "Zena is also beautiful." We looked at each other, knowing the pain we had shared, knowing the joy of being mother and daughter and friends, sharing one soul that had been cut into halves, four long years ago, but now rejoined; however, our bodies no longer fit together as when I was a child.

I wondered what Father had told her. Did she know that I wanted to leave Africa and go to America, possibly never returning? If he had, I could not tell. Her face was worn. At age thirty, Zena seemed older than Mother Stevens who was forty-two. Gray hair had woven into her cornrows. She had many more lines, deep-set in her forehead. Her chaffed cheeks had never known the luxury of lotion.

Zena and I walked to Mother Stevens's house.

"Then she will not go," my father said.

"Mr. Sackey, please, listen to reason," Mother Stevens said. She stood in the living room. There were couches, but Mother Stevens never invited people to sit on her peach-colored cushions. She held a clipboard in one hand and a black Bic pen in the other. Father towered above her. She offered the pen to Father. She faced him with resolve and a sternness that I knew well. In a rare defeat, Mother Stevens withdrew the offer of the pen to Father.

"I raised her as *my* daughter, and *I* gave her a proper English name." Mother Stevens shook her head as if she were in disbelief. "Seriously, how do you expect her to go to America as *Jabonkah Sackey*? The other children will make fun of that name. She must have a proper name to assimilate." She paused. "Fit in." She created another moment of silence, then said, "Do you know what would happen if she does *not* go as an immigrant?" Mother lifted her chin in the air to stare at Father. "They will force her to come back to Africa once her student visa expires, then what? Are you so short-sighted? Really, I am helping this poor girl," she paused, "and you never did."

Father stretched even taller and crossed his arms, eyes closed to slits, jaw clenched with muscles bulging. His white shirt was soaked with sweat and clung to his chest. We all waited for Father to loosen his jaw and speak.

One of the men from the village held the screen door open. I was surprised that Mother Stevens didn't yell at him as she did others who held it open. Flies entered the house, more than usual, as if they were attracted to something; perhaps the smell of meat, which we had all eaten. Zena shuffled closer to my side.

Mother Stevens broke the silence, "Why be so unreasonable, when she," Mother Stevens nodded toward me, "has been Jeanette Stevens for these many years?"

No change in Father.

"You didn't want her. Remember?" Mother Stevens said with a bite in her voice. She continued, "You said that she was worthless. Or do you deny this?"

Father took a quick glance at me, then snapped back to his former, ridged posture.

"You said I could have her and you never wanted to see her again." She seemed her usual self now, commanding, inflexible.

"You should have adopted her," Father said, finally, with a grumble, "if you wanted her to have your name." He poked a finger at Mother Stevens. "You should have done it legally. Instead, you stole my name from her."

Mother Stevens pulled her head back. "Sir, there is no need to be hostile. We are both civilized people. You must be flexible."

The more Mother Stevens resisted Father, the more hope I bled. I had never known Father to be flexible. I was about to speak up, but Zena took my hand and squeezed hard until my bones ground together with mouth-closing pain.

"I gave her a Christian education. Tell me, Mr. Sackey, what have you done for her?"

So many memories came to my mind, all terrible and painful, reflecting on Father and the pain he had given to Zena and me. Zena twisted my hand. My thoughts returned to the present. With her silence, Zena said, "Man rules."

But here at the mission, Mother Stevens ruled. Inside me, I cheered for her, repenting my stubbornness, forgiving her for all of the whippings she had given me. She had to rule. She had to win Father over.

Both Mother Stevens and Father were made of hard clay, neither moving from their stubbornness. I wanted to speak up, but Zena's constant pressure kept my mouth shut, even though my hopes for leaving Africa were nearly drained. I needed to tell Mother Stevens it was okay to be Jabonkah Sackey. I wanted to scream at Father to stop being impossible.

"Okay," Mother Stevens said.

I gasped. Everyone looked at me. Zena held my hand so tightly I feared she would break it if I made another noise.

"How about Jeanette Sackey?" She held the pen to Father, nearly touching him on the nose, causing his eyes to cross.

He snatched the pen from Mother. "American women are so stubborn, *Jabonkah* is already like them. She should feel at home." He reached for the clipboard.

Mother Stevens didn't allow him to grab it but held it back. She was making him say please, something he would never do. Mother Stevens offered it to him slowly. He grabbed at it when it was within reach and yanked it out of her hand.

His eyes narrowed. He seemed to read the document. He scribbled and wrote on the paper. His last name, no doubt. He handed it back to Mother Stevens, and Zena released the horrible squeezing pressure. My hopes returned. With each relieved breath I took, I felt an increasing sense of gratefulness to Mother Stevens and Father. I grabbed Zena and hugged her.

She took my hand, the one that she had squeezed so hard, brought it to her lips, then kissed it. With my head on Zena's shoulder, I watched Father duck out the doorway and walk outside. His two men followed him.

I saw Father for what he was—Father. I thought he had only hated Zena and me. He might hate all women. Why did he? Why do snakes eat the helpless frogs? Maybe Father lived according to his nature. Yet he had just acted against his nature, for me, with the bold assistance of Mother Stevens, of course.

As Mother Stevens passed Zena and me, she said, "You can change your name to Stevens when you become a citizen."

Mother Stevens ruled, I thought.

# 45

# An X Bigger Than Africa

Before the sun was up, Zena shook me. I had hardly slept. We had lain together on my little bed. Zena had seemed to sleep deeply. There had been no room to move unless we both did. I hadn't cared.

There had been many things to think about. What had repeated all night long was my leaving Bomi Hills, the bush, the animals, the smell of rice, the red clay, the rain, the sunshine, and Africa, the land of my childhood.

Going to America meant leaving Zena, the person I loved the most. I remembered our times of joy and times of pain. I knew this was in the past. I needed my own life. Zena had a new life that was free from Father.

It had taken a lot of gestures and laughter, and Mother Stevens had hushed us several times, yet we continued to giggle, until finally I had understood—Zena had left Father but remained in our village, with his consent I gathered, and he had even given her a hut of her own. He had, most likely, replaced Zena with a younger wife.

This revelation was so powerful, so profound, it had stunned me with disbelief. She was free of "the man rules," and I was soon to be free of

"Mother Stevens's rule." We had hugged even more, and our laughter had turned to quiet sobs of joy. Finally, Mother Stevens had risen from her bed and came to my room to scold us. I had been fearful that she would whip Zena and me. She hadn't.

How could I sleep? I felt great relief. I had finally decided I could leave Africa, knowing Zena was free. Zena and I were two birds of the bush— driven away—free from the cruel rule of others.

We rose. The boys needed their breakfast. We started a fire under the big black pot to cook oats, then we bathed, quickly, in cold water, using Mother Stevens's special water, which Zena seemed to enjoy drinking more than bathing in.

After breakfast, the driver of the big black car came to take Mother Stevens, Zena, Father, and me to Monrovia. Mother Stevens said that Father and Zena had to sign more papers, which made Father unhappy, but he seemed to like being with Mother Stevens. I was not certain, but I thought Mother Stevens enjoyed being with him.

Red dust billowed in windows each time the car slowed for turns, for deep holes in the road, or for women with large bundles on their heads. No one talked, but Mother Stevens hummed hymns that I hummed with her. Zena also hummed. She sounded more like she was ill and moaned with a fever. I didn't laugh, which took great effort. I smiled instead.

We arrived outside a large building. We all got out. Mother Stevens lectured the driver to wait by the market. Apparently, she wanted to shop while we were in the city. She walked quickly, not waiting for any of us to climb the stairs or walk the long hallways. She never looked back. No one would have thought we were together. Father was the closest to her, attempting to stay close, but he had difficulty forcing his way down the crowded hallway, unlike Mother Stevens who seemed not to care if she bumped people and cut off their paths.

I held Zena's hand while I led us, politely, through those who seemed lost and confused by the many doors we all passed; I read the names on the offices, which were in large black letters on blurry glass. Once we finally caught up with them, Mother Stevens and Father were talking, standing by the door with letters that read: VISAS AND PASSPORTS.

"Please, Mr. Sackey, you are a man of business and intelligence." Father smiled briefly, but it faded when Mother Stevens continued, "So don't be as obstinate as you were about Jeanette's name."

I thought that if Father's black face had been white, it would have been tomato red. Father opened the door and went inside. He didn't wait for the rest of us or hold the door open. Mother Stevens let the door close in her face. We stood and waited. Finally, Father opened the door and Mother Stevens slipped past him, as if he were being a gentleman, acknowledging her as a lady. Zena and I didn't let Father see our smiles.

There was a long line inside. Fans above our heads turned in circles, like pinwheels in the wind, like the ones the boys brought with them to school.

After we waited in line, an elderly man with round glasses, who sat behind the biggest desk I had ever seen, greeted us. It would take four or five of Mother Stevens's desk or two of those at the bank to equal his. Four chairs sat opposite the old man. Mother Stevens scooted her chair closer. The man's shirt was so white that it made Father's shirt appear soiled.

Father sat on Mother Stevens's left. I sat to her right and Zena to my right. A red cord, which hung the length of the man's desk, held the people back who were next in line. They pushed against the rope and stared at us. The elderly man with the round glasses left us sitting and went behind a door. He came back with a tan folder, like one Mother Stevens used to keep her papers. The man's folder was new and not stuffed with unruly papers, like hers.

The man sat, opened the file, took out the documents, then spread them in front of him. After studying them, he looked up at me. His eyes were magnified and seemed twice the size of normal eyes.

"You are Jeanette Stevens?"

I nodded.

Father burst out, "She is Jabonkah Sackey!"

The man's eyes grew even larger.

Mother Stevens grasped Father's right arm and said, "Please, please, Mr. Sackey, let me handle this." Father hesitated, but finally he sat back in his chair. She removed her hand from his arm, then scooted forward, laid her old folder on the desk, and opened it.

She selected the top paper, the one I thought Father had signed, and laid it on the table, twisted it, and pushed it toward the man across from her. "Mr....?"

"Adams."

Mother Stevens and Mr. Adams shook hands.

"Mr. Adams, this is Jeanette's father, John Henry Sackey." Mother looked at Father, then Father and Mr. Adams shook hands. "This is Mrs. Sackey." Zena shook the offered hand. "And this, of course, is Jeanette..." Mother Stevens paused, jumping up slightly, pulling on the skirt beneath her bottom, "Jeanette Sackey." Father relaxed his rigid frame and slouched.

I tried to understand what Mr. Adams and Mother Stevens were talking about, but it was as useless as trying to figure out what Zena had said to me in Gola.

Mr. Adams handed Zena a pen to sign a paper he had pushed in front of her. She frowned. She shook her head then gazed at me. I smiled and nodded. I took the paper that she was to sign and positioned it before her. I gripped Zena's hand, helping her hold the pen until it pointed above the line next to her name, where she was supposed to sign. Still with my hand over hers, we drew an X that was bigger than Africa. She smiled and seemed proud of herself. She was eager to make more Xs, which we did again another three times during our visit with Mr. Adams.

# 46
# I Will Miss Africa

The sunset glowed bright red and set fire to the clouds. A hawk circled over my head, searching the clearing for his dinner. I rested high above the bush on a skinny palm. The continual onshore winds had shaped the tree's body into a deformed curve, which resembled a shepherd's hook. It must have been weaker than the tall, straight palms that towered beside it. Someday, a violent gale might bend it too far and break it. I wrapped my legs and arms around it in a hug. It was a position that I could hold forever, enough of my weight rested on the trunk that it made my clinging effortless.

After not having seen Zena for four years, I only had gotten to be with her for three days, because Father had wanted to leave the next morning after the papers had been signed. On that morning, we hadn't wanted to let go of each other. We had cried and cried and cried. Mother Stevens had forced her arms around my waist, and Father had yanked Zena's shoulders in a mean way. Zena and I had struggled, but they had eventually separated us. Our arms had remained stretched out for the other, as our cries grew fainter, and the distance between us grew too great. I hadn't dropped my arms until Zena became a short shadow on the road that led back to the bush. Zena's departure left me with a greater sense of loneliness than before.

Growing up I had never longed to live a different day, never longed to be anywhere else, to be anyone else, nor needed anybody except Zena. It was after Father had given me away that I had come to know longing, wishing for another day, even before the sun had set on the current one. I had become desperate to be another person.

But now, I could be myself, Jabonkah—the one God remembered. He had taken more time than termites needed to eat a log. Mother Stevens had reminded me that I still didn't have a sponsor. I had a place to stay with Mother Moore—that was settled. I needed a sponsor who would be financially responsible for me.

Not that I understood what a sponsor was, but it gave Mother Stevens a long face. Mine had to be longer. I rested my cheek against the smooth bark of the palm tree. I prayed little soft prayers, mostly repeating please, please, please. A hawk screeched as it flapped its wings, climbing high, talons empty, missing the snatch of its prey.

Mother Stevens reminded me this was a troubled time for the youth in America. She said that in the days before Vietnam and something called hippies, her home church in Oakland would have sponsored me solely on her recommendation. She understood their current concerns but didn't agree. Just because two teens in their congregation had become pregnant didn't mean I would be as foolish.

The wind cooled my sweaty body. I sighed and hugged the tree tighter, feeling a little dizzy, looking at the same ground the hawk hunted for its supper.

I slipped down the palm. I walked slowly back to the mission in the last bit of dusk. My head drooped like the hawk's, but I was not looking for a mouse to eat. I needed a sponsor, someone who trusted me not to let a boy have me. Boys! Why would any girl do that?

"Jeanette!" Mother called for me.

What had I forgotten? I went through the list: boys fed, bowls and pots cleaned, her water, her dinner, her pot? Had I forgotten to empty her pot? No, I remembered the snakes in the rafters had been missing today, and I had felt relieved. It was too early for her bath. What? My steps slowed. The boys that were near looked at me as if they were happy that I, and not them, was about to get a beating.

"Jeanette, where are you?" Mother Stevens persisted. "You have a sponsor!"

I lifted my head and ran, knees pumping high in the air, jumping over logs, dashing through and around groups of boys who cheered for me. They knew every bit of my hopes and needs.

Mother Stevens stood in her doorway, a letter in her hand. It was the same kind of stationary that Mother Moore used. Mother Stevens was smiling. "Viola has answered our prayers. God has laid his will on her heart, and she prayed about it and spoke to the elders, and now she has written," she waved the letter that was in her hand, "informing me she is willing to mortgage her house to fulfill the financial obligations as your sponsor." She put her hands together and raised them to the sky. "Thank you, Lord Jesus."

I jumped and shouted, repeating, "Thank you, Lord Jesus," along with Mother Stevens. The boys gathered and started jumping and praising God with us, until we were all in a frenzy of praise. Several boys grabbed me and lifted me in the air. I heard Mother Stevens yelling for them to be careful not to hurt me. She laughed when I began to scream. The boys passed me around, still over their heads, for the most part, many hands touching and grabbing me to keep me from falling, tickling and hurting at the same time.

Finally, I relaxed. I spread my arms and legs, making it easier for them to heft and pass me over their heads. I giggled and laughed. This went on until Mother Stevens stopped it. Someone had started a fire, a large one. The boys gathered around, removing their shirts, singing and chanting songs of Africa, songs of the bush from their different tribes, dancing their unique dances.

I sat at Mother Stevens's feet on the porch of her house. We watched the boys pretending to be men, beating rhythms with sticks on logs, on rocks, on cans, on anything that would make noise.

"Will you miss this?" Mother said.

I was not sure what she meant—would I miss the boys, the work, the mission, or her? None of these things I would miss. Her foot kept beat with the pounding sticks. She rocked gently back and forth. The boys of Africa danced and cried out songs that made them happy. They danced and feigned hunting and killing large beasts.

"Yes, ma'am, I will miss Africa."

# 47

# I Was Only Your Daughter

It was December 20, 1964. My flight was scheduled to take off at 11:00 a.m. from Monrovia. I woke early, just as I had these past four years, but today I didn't have to feed the boys. Mother Stevens had hired two women from the Bassa tribe to cook and clean up.

My morning devotions consisted of songs of praise as joy filled my heart completely. I didn't care if I woke the entire mission. After my songs, I bathed, scrubbing every inch of my body. I had cut a lime in half. I squeezed the juice into my hands and rubbed it under my arms.

Mother Stevens had bought me a new dress and shoes. The dress hung heavy. It was made of thick cotton. It was pretty, a large floral print with long sleeves that had lace around the wrists. This would help keep me warm, she had said, because it was winter in Oakland. She had also bought a sweater that would drive the cold away, something I could hardly imagine.

The shoes were size six and a half—pumps; Mother Stevens called them—and were an inch and a half too small. The cramped pain in my toes was not a concern, considering where these shoes were going to take me. Of course, I didn't say anything to her. I feared the slightest complaint might cause her to change her mind about sending me to America.

She had allowed me to wear the shoes but not the dress. I had told Randy about my dilemma, and he had suggested filling the shoes partway with sand and walking around, trying to lengthen them. I suffered many blisters and finally decided I would not be able to walk before these shoes stretched.

Today, Mother Stevens expected me for breakfast. She had put a white cloth over her dining room table. She had cut red roses and put them in a vase in the center. This was the first and last time we ate together.

Mother Stevens sighed. "I don't know where to start." She sighed again, deeper. "Sit up straight."

I leaned back and made my legs long until my body was like a limb without bends or curves. My head rested on the back of the chair.

"No, no, heavens no," Mother Stevens said as she laughed. "Sit up in your chair."

I quickly got up and stood on my chair straight like a ruler.

By now, Mother Stevens was having difficulty breathing. She held her middle and began to cry. She was trying to teach me something that I didn't understand. I sat in the chair.

"Oh, dear me," Mother Stevens took a breath, "I had no idea you were so ignorant of table manners."

This hurt my feelings.

"But that is okay. I will send Viola a letter and explain that it is my fault you are not a lady."

This also hurt my feelings. I had always wanted to be a lady like Miss Palmer from the bank, but Mother Stevens was so happy I could not stay upset. I smiled with her.

Zena and Father arrived at the mission while I was getting dressed. Mother Stevens would not allow Zena in the house. Zena stood near the window, watching Mother Stevens make new cornrows in my hair. Zena had learned the word "pretty" and kept repeating it.

*Why can't she come in?* I wanted to ask Mother Stevens but feared she would become angry. She was already jerking and pulling too hard on my hair. I did ask, "Are we going to be late, ma'am?"

"We will if you don't hold still."

But I was holding still! I wondered what time it was. I couldn't see the clock on her desk. I began to fret. My stomach had knots in it. I felt like screaming.

"There. Now get your suitcase and don't forget the x-rays."

"Why do I need them?"

"I already told you a dozen times," Mother Stevens said. "Just don't offer them. Keep them out of sight when you get to New York and go through customs."

I still didn't understand what customs was but recognized the level of concern on her face, which meant I needed to do as she said.

"Keep the films out of your suitcase, because they will dump everything out; they will see them and give them to the health official who reads them."

"What if—?"

"Jeanette, if it is God's will for you to be in America, then they will not read your x-rays."

I took the large packet that held the black and grey films and tucked it under my arm, then picked up my tattered suitcase. Mother Stevens and I walked outside together. The boys began to cheer, and many came to shake my hand or hug me. Zena stood next to the crowd of boys, waving, smiling, lips saying, "Pretty."

Mother Stevens took me by the arm and forced her way through the boys.

"Wait. Wait. I want to say goodbye to Zena," I said, worried that we would be separated.

Mother Stevens tugged harder. "She and your Father will be at the airport; now come along."

The car traveled faster than normal and bumped us around. Mother Stevens told the driver to hurry up instead of slow down, as she would have in any case other than being late for my plane. She sat in the front with both hands on the dash. She complained that the dash was hot, even though she had white gloves on, like mine. Hers were prettier, but I didn't care. These were my first pair.

We raced on the smooth streets of Monrovia. Mother Stevens kept checking her watch, which made me very nervous. At the airport, she dragged me through the big terminal building and spoke to the security man, who had a large gun. He gave us permission to pass with the other people who held tickets in their hands.

Outside, I heard my name being called, "Jabonkah! Jabonkah!"

Lined along the gate seemed to be all of the people from my village.

Some I remembered, and others I didn't. Father stood above everyone, but Zena was not there, nor was she hidden behind the others. I dropped my suitcase and ran to the metal fence that held them.

Mother Stevens yelled, "Jeanette, come here." But I didn't look back.

Father pressed against the fence, but Zena was still nowhere in sight. "Where is she?" I said to Father.

His eyes were as I had never seen them, relaxed on the edges, blinking quickly, looking behind me at the huge airplane and back at me. "She couldn't watch you leave," he said finally. He breathed deeply then placed the palm of his hand against the squares of the silver fence. Only violence had come from that hand: whippings, beatings, hard fists to my face.

I raised my left arm. His eyes narrowed, but his hand remained. I pressed my left hand against the flesh of his. "I am not a witch. I was only your daughter." I dropped my arm, turned, and ran away. Afraid that he would somehow grab me from behind, I ran as fast as my bunched up dress and painful toes allowed.

I stopped in front of Mother Stevens and looked up at her. "I hate him."

She turned her head in the direction of Father. "Yes, I know." She stuck a gloved finger under my chin and lifted it. "Only the power of God can heal our deepest wounds." She let my chin go, and then took my hand.

With my suitcase and x-rays, I got in line with Mother Stevens. She held my ticket. When we got to the beautiful black woman who had blue paint above her eyes and whose eye lashes were longer than any I had seen before, she took my ticket from Mother Stevens.

"May I go on board with her? It's the first time she has flown," Mother Stevens said.

The pretty woman said, "Yes, of course."

The inside of the airplane smelled of cigarette smoke, and the air was cold. We had left my bag at the stairs where men put my bag on a moving tongue that stuck into the belly of the airplane. Mother Stevens kept looking above me for something and at the ticket piece that the woman had handed back to her.

"Here we are, Jeanette, your seat. Look here." She pointed to the letter and numbers C53, and then to the remainder of my ticket that had the same letter and numbers. "This is your seat." She paused. "Go ahead, you may sit down."

She reached across my lap and found a blue strap with a silver piece of metal on the end. She grabbed a second one and pressed them together with a click. "Jeanette." Mother Stevens knelt beside me, removed her gloves and mine, and grasped my hands in hers. She said, "You have been...a...," her eyes were full of tears, "...good and faithful servant."

My eyes blurred. I said, "I love you, and I am sorry for all the times I made you cross and...and...and I thank you for all the beatings you gave me. I...was a bad girl."

"No, no, you were a good girl, my darling." She hugged me. I hugged her. She cried. I cried, until the pretty woman told her she had to leave the plane. Mother Stevens kissed me on the forehead, and then placed her hands on top of my head.

"Heavenly Father, keep this child safe from harm and deliver her safely to Miss Moore, who is a blessed saint for her generosity."

She kissed me on the cheek and softly said, "Please forgive me." She turned and left. I tried to get out of my seat, but the blue strap held tight. I figured out how to unbuckle it and crawled over the two empty seats to look out the window. Mother Stevens walked quickly to the terminal. Father waved from behind the fence.

# 48

# Customs

Back in my seat, the pretty stewardess re-buckled me, then left and returned with a cola that had been poured over ice cubes.

"Thank you, ma'am. My name is Jeanette Sackey, what's yours?" She was the most beautiful woman I had seen since Miss Palmer, and she smelled like roses.

She pointed to a strip of plastic on her white blouse and said, extending her delicate hand, "I'm pleased to meet you, Jeanette. My name is Betty." After we shook hands, she said, "I'll have to take your drink back before we take off, but enjoy it for now."

Enjoy I did. I stuck my nose close to the brown liquid and let the bubbles tickle my nose. It reminded me that I was not dreaming. I had never dreamed about my nose tickling and being splashed with tiny drops of wetness.

The plane began to rumble. I looked around for Betty. She was far away, helping passengers with pillows and blankets. It was cold, but I didn't mind; this, too, reminded me that I was not dreaming.

Betty did finally come to me, and she looked at my cola. "You weren't thirsty?" I had not drunk any of it. She reached down with the back of her hand and wiped my nose. Her brow wrinkled. "What's wrong, Jeanette?"

I looked up and grinned, possibly the biggest grin in my life. "Nothing. I'm going to America." I handed her my cup; it was still full, but the ice was almost gone.

"Baby, you keep that drink," Betty said, then moved on to tend to other passengers.

Soon we began to move, and these terrible whining noises filled the inside of the airplane. I wanted to cover my ears, so I drank my cola then used both hands to block the noise. This could not be a dream! The plane ran fast then swayed back and forth as the ground drew further away. My stomach had the most exciting feeling, similar to when I played on the monkey bridge. I unbuckled and scrambled to the window seat.

I was amazed at how my country seemed so flat and green, with brown patches where huts were grouped into villages. I gripped the arms of the seat as the plane tilted to the left. All I saw was the bluest sky. I squeezed my legs together, fearing I might pee. After months of worry and waiting, I was going to America!

After the plane leveled, I could see the ocean on the left side and the African bush on my right side. Betty came and checked on me frequently, giving me permission to change seats for now, so I could look out the window, but when we landed in Morocco, she said that I would have to go back to my seat.

When we landed, Betty let me get off the airplane. I went straight away and bought a new pair of shoes with part of the money Mother Stevens had given me. Back on the plane, a white man in a flowery short-sleeved shirt sat in the window seat. I minded my own business as Mother Stevens had scolded me about, so I didn't talk to him. I did look past him, once we were in the air; perhaps too much so, because he offered to switch seats with me, which I did almost before he could unbuckle.

For hours I watched the ocean and checked where the sky and ocean fit together. The white man slept. I was tired, but I kept pinching my face and the back of my arm where the skin is tender to keep from falling into the same breathing rhythm as the man next to me. Although I knew that I could never imagine a dream like this, I refused to sleep.

Betty came by and whispered, "Come and eat." She offered her hand.

"You can leave your gloves in the seat."

She led me up the stairs where there was a table with food on it. She told me that this was for those in first-class seating, but since I was a special passenger, I could eat here. She assured me that I could eat as many hamburgers as I wanted, which I did. I made several trips back to first class and even offered to get a hamburger for the man next to me, but he didn't want one.

At night it was especially difficult to stay awake, though I managed to. It was easy to stay awake when we got over New York City, because the lights were so beautiful. I wanted to share the joy with the man next to me, but he seemed to have no interest and no longer smiled.

Betty helped me get off the plane and told me to just follow the others who were in line for customs. Customs! I had forgotten about customs and the x-rays. I waited with my bag and packet of black-and-grey films. Soon, it was my turn to come close to the man who was looking in passengers' bags. I heard him ask the people whose bags they searched if they had anything to declare. That scared me, so I fell back, deeper in line.

Finally, there was no more line to fall back into; I was next. I looked up at the soldier-appearing man in his green uniform and golden badge. "Passport."

He looked at me like any man in Liberia looks at a girl child—through me. I had put my passport in the packet with the x-rays. My legs felt weak. My knees went soft. "It's in my suitcase!" I knew it was a lie, but I felt that I had to help God's will.

While he grabbed my suitcase and began to search through it, I turned my back to him and slipped the passport out of the packet that held the x-rays. "Oh, here it is." I offered him my passport with my left hand and hid the x-rays behind my back with my right hand.

He closed the lid on my suitcase and snapped the buttons, then took my passport, stamped it, and handed it back to me.

"Move on, miss."

I only had one hand, and it had my passport in it. I froze. I could not grasp it with the same hand that held the passport.

His eyebrows came together. "Something wrong, miss?" He seemed to be suspicious. He stepped back and looked behind me, but I turned as he moved.

Straightening, he held out his hand. I handed him the packet with the x-rays. "Please, sir, don't send me back to Africa. I have prayed and prayed and prayed for this day and now, Mother Stevens said," I grabbed his free hand, "that if it was God's will for me to come to America that he would open the door for me."

His eyes said, "No." Then he turned my hands over and rubbed his fingers over the palm of my left hand. His eyes changed, opened and relaxed. "Uncle Sam has a will of his own, miss."

I had no idea who Uncle Sam was, but he could not be more important than God, I thought. "Please, sir."

"Where are you headed? Where's your ticket?"

"It's with the...x-rays."

He removed the ticket, looked at it, then checked the time on his watch. "No time to get public health to see you." He smiled then said, "Welcome to America. Now go, hurry; you have a long way to get to your gate."

Relief from passing customs turned to horror when I thought that I might miss my flight to San Francisco. Though it was late evening, the terminal was packed with people who were very tall and white. I had never seen so many of them. Few even looked at me. I felt as if I were just a drop of mist.

"Are you lost?" It was a policeman, a black man.

"Yes, yes, sir. I'm Jeanette Sackey, and I'm going to San Francisco." I pointed to my chest. Betty had written this on a piece of tan tape and pasted it to my dress.

"Well, young lady, you won't get there standing around." He looked up at the giant board with names and numbers on it. He mumbled, "American Airlines," then said, "It's the only carrier headed there at this hour." He checked my ticket. He grabbed my suitcase. "Keep up, okay?"

He had long legs, so I had to take many steps, at least two steps for his one. We rushed and rushed and rushed until we stopped at a counter where smiling ladies looked down on me.

The policeman handed them my ticket and pointed to my tape. "This is Jeanette Sackey, and she's going to San Francisco."

"Well, you got here just in time. We were about to close the door."

Now in my seat, I said to a man who wore a blue uniform with red stripes down his left sleeve and who sat in the window seat, "May I sit where you are, sir?"

He looked at me for a moment with his blurry eyes and said, "Sure thing, miss."

We changed seats, and he talked for the longest time about ships and the American Navy and how he was being transferred to San Francisco to his new ship. He was drunk, but he didn't smell like he had been drinking palm wine.

Stars, long patches of darkness, then a small cluster of lights appeared. So many villages had electricity. I refused to sleep, still fearing that I might wake from this dream. We began to be tossed around, and rain slid sideways across my window as we came from high above and were about to land.

The sailor man didn't wake up. I was tempted to reach over and hold his hand. He woke when we jolted on the ground. He took the Lord's name in vain then said, "Beg your pardon, miss." He grinned. He was handsome.

Soon we were allowed to leave the airplane. I stood in line for the stairs that went way up high to where we were to get our bags. People massed above us looking down. I sensed that Mother Moore was there waiting for me, but I could not see her, not that I would have known what she looked like. I fixed onto the black female faces until one waved at me.

It had to be Viola Moore. She was slender. She wore a long black coat and held a red umbrella in her hand. At the stairs, I jumped back. They were moving. They had teeth. They had people on them, and the people seemed okay. Mother Moore came close to the top of the moving stairs and waved for me to come to her. I shook my head and waved for her to come and get me. People behind me began to say rude things and grumbled.

Then a man picked me up and swooped me into his strong arms. It was the man in blue, the sailor. Cheers and clapping erupted from behind and above. I squirmed a little, then focused on Mother Moore, her smooth kind face and her open arms that dangled her umbrella.

At the top of the stairs, the sailor put me down in front of Mother Moore. "I'm Jeanette."

She smiled the biggest smile and said, "Yes, you are, and now you are my daughter." We hugged and hugged and hugged until there were no others around us.

# The End

Jeanette Mills
"Jabonkah Sackey"
2012

Made in the USA
Lexington, KY
21 May 2013